A
VERY
EASY
DEATH

Books by Simone de Beauvoir

A Very Easy Death
All Said And Done
The Coming of Age

Published by
WARNER BOOKS

A VERY EASY DEATH

Simone de Beauvoir

Translated from the French
by Patrick O'Brian

WARNER BOOKS

A Warner Communications Company

WARNER BOOKS EDITION

© 1964 by Librairie Gallimard
First published in Paris under the title
Une Mort Très Douce
English translation © 1965 by Andre Deutsch Ltd.,
George Weidenfeld and Nicolson Ltd., and G.P. Putnam's Sons.
All rights reserved. This book or parts thereof must not be
reproduced in any form without permission.

Library of Congress Catalog Card Number: 66-15581

ISBN 0-446-89441-9

This Warner Books Edition is published by
arrangement with G.P. Putnam's Sons, Inc.

Cover design by M. Houner

Warner Books, Inc., 75 Rockefeller Plaza, New York, N.Y. 10019

A Warner Communications Company

Printed in the United States of America

Not associated with Warner Press, Inc. of Anderson, Indiana

First Printing: August, 1973

Reissued: July, 1977

10 9 8 7 6 5 4 3 2

For my sister

Do not go gentle into that good night.
Old age should burn and rave at close of day;
Rage, rage against the dying of the light . . .

DYLAN THOMAS

A
VERY
EASY
DEATH

AT FOUR O'CLOCK in the afternoon of Thursday, 24 October 1963, I was in Rome, in my room at the Hotel Minerva; I was to fly home the next day and I was putting papers away when the telephone rang. It was Bost calling me from Paris: 'Your mother has had an accident,' he said. I thought: she has been knocked down by a car; she was climbing laboriously from the roadway to the pavement, leaning on her stick, and a car knocked her down. 'She had a fall in the bathroom: she has broken the neck of her femur,' said Bost. He lived in the same building as my mother. About ten o'clock the evening before, he had been going up the stairs with Olga, and they noticed three people ahead of them—a woman and two policemen. 'It's the landing above the second floor,' the woman was saying. Had .something happened to Madame de Beauvoir? Yes. A fall. For two hours she had crawled across the floor before she could reach the telephone; she had asked a friend, Madame Tardieu, to have the door forced open. Bost and Olga followed them up to the flat. They found Maman lying on the floor in her red corduroy dressing-gown. Dr

Lacroix, a woman doctor who was living in the house, diagnosed a fracture of the neck of the femur: Maman had been taken away by the emergency service of the Boucicaut hospital and she spent the night in the public ward. 'But I'm taking her to the C nursing home,' Bost told me. 'That's where Professor B operates—he's one of the best bone surgeons. She was against it; she was afraid it would cost you too much. But I persuaded her in the end.'

Poor Maman! I had lunched with her when I came back from Moscow five weeks before; she looked poorly, as usual. There had been a time, not very long ago, when she took pleasure in the thought that she did not look her age; now there could no longer be any mistake about it—she was a woman of seventy-seven, quite worn out. The arthritis in her hips, which had first appeared after the war, had grown worse year by year, in spite of massage and cures at Aix-les-Bains; it took her an hour to make her way round one block of houses. She had a good deal of pain and she slept badly in spite of the six aspirins she took every day. For the last two or three years, and especially since the last winter, I had always seen her with those dark rings round her eyes, her face thin and a pinched look about her nose. It was nothing serious, said D, her doctor—an upset liver and sluggish bowels. He prescribed some drugs: tamarind jelly for constipation. That day I had not been surprised at her feeling poorly; what did upset me was that she should have had a bad summer. She could have taken a holiday in a country hotel or a convent that took boarders. But she expected to be asked to stay at Meyrignac by my cousin Jeanne, as she was every year, and at Scharrachbergen, where my sister lived. Both of them were prevented from inviting her. So she stayed on in Paris; it rained, and the town was deserted. 'I'm never depressed, as you know,' she said to me, 'but I was depressed then.' Fortunately, a little while after I passed through, my sister had had her to stay in Alsace for a fortnight. Now her friends were in Paris again; I was coming back; and but for that broken bone I should certainly have found her in good form once more. Her heart was in excellent condition and her bloodpressure was that of a young woman: I had never been afraid of a sudden mishap for her.

At about six o'clock I telephoned her at the nursing home. I told her that I was on my way back and that I was coming to see her. She answered in a wavering, doubtful voice. Professor B took over the telephone: he was going to operate on Saturday morning.

'You haven't written me a letter for two months!' she said, as I came towards her bed. I protested: we had seen each other; I had sent her a letter from Rome. She listened to me with an air of disbelief. Her forehead and hands were burning hot; her mouth was slightly twisted, she had difficulty in articulating and her mind was confused. Was this the effect of shock? Or had her fall been caused by a slight stroke? She had always had a nervous tic. (No, not always, but for a long while. Since when?) She blinked; her eyebrows went up, her forehead wrinkled. While I was there, this nervous movement never stopped for a second. And when her smooth, rounded eyelids came down they completely covered her pupils. Dr J, an assistant, looked in: there was no point in operating; the femur had not shifted, and with three months of rest it would re-knit. Maman seemed relieved. In a muddled way she told me about her efforts to reach the telephone, her intense anxiety; the kindness of Bost and Olga. She had been taken to the hospital in her dressing-gown, without any baggage at all. The next day Olga had brought her toilet things, some eau de Cologne and a pretty white wool bed-jacket. When she said thank you Olga had replied, 'But I do it out of affection, Madame.' Several times, with an earnest, musing air, Maman repeated, 'She said to me, "I do it out of affection."'

'She seemed so ashamed of being a nuisance, so immensely grateful for what was done for her: it was enough to break your heart,' Olga told me that evening. She spoke indignantly of Dr D. He was annoyed at Dr Lacroix's having been called in and he had refused to go and see Maman at the hospital on Thursday. 'I stood there clutching the telephone for twenty minutes,' said Olga. 'After the shock and after her night in the hospital, your mother needed comforting by her usual doctor. He wouldn't listen to a word of it.' Bost did not think that Maman had had a stroke: when he had helped her up she seemed a little bewildered but quite clear in her mind. He doubted whether she would recover in three months, however: the breaking of the neck of the femur was not in itself a serious matter, but a long period of lying still caused bed-sores, and with old people they did not heal. The lying position was tiring for the lungs: patients developed pneumonia and it carried them off. I was not very much affected. In spite of her frailty my mother was tough. And after all, she was of an age to die.

Bost had told my sister, and I had a long talk with her on the telephone. 'I knew it would happen!' she said. In Alsace she had thought Maman had aged so and had grown so weak that she had said to Lionel, 'She will never get through the winter.' One night Maman had had violent abdominal pains: she had very nearly asked to be taken to hospital. But in the morning she was better. And when they took her home by car, 'charmed, delighted with her stay', as she put it, she had recovered her strength and her cheerfulness. But half-way through October, about ten days before her accident, Francine Diato telephoned my sister. 'I have just been having lunch with your mother. She seemed to me so poorly that I thought I ought to warn you.' My sister invented an excuse for coming to Paris at once, and she took Maman to a radiologist. When he had looked at the plates her doctor stated categorically, 'There is nothing for you to worry about. A kind of pocket has formed in the intestine, a faecal pocket that makes the movement of the bowels difficult. And then your mother does not eat enough, which could cause deficiencies; but she is in no danger.' He advised Maman to feed herself better and prescribed her new and very strongly-acting medicines. 'But I was still worried,' said Poupette. 'I begged Maman to have someone in at night. She never would: she could not bear the idea of a strange woman sleeping in her flat.' Poupette and I agreed that she should come to Paris in a fortnight's time, when I planned to leave for Prague.

The next day Maman's mouth was still twisted and her speech somewhat troubled; her long eyelids were drooping over her eyes, and her eyebrows twitched. Her right arm, which she had broken twenty years before, falling off a bicycle, had never mended properly; her recent fall had hurt her left arm: she could scarcely move either of them. Fortunately, she was being looked after with the greatest care. Her room overlooked a garden, far from the noise of the street. Her bed had been moved, and they had put it along the wall that ran parallel to the window so that the telephone, which was fixed to the wall, was within hand's reach. With her back propped up with pillows, she was sitting rather than lying: her lungs would not get tired. Her pneumatic mattress, connected to an electrical device, vibrated, massaging her: this was to prevent bed-sores. Every morning a physiotherapist came and exercised her legs. It seemed as if the dangers Bost had spoken of could be averted. In her rather drowsy voice Maman told me that a maid cut up her meat and helped her to eat, and that the meals were excellent. Whereas at the hospital they had given her black pudding and potatoes! 'Black pudding! For invalids!' She talked more easily than on the day before. She went back over the two dreadful hours when she was dragging herself across the floor, wondering whether she would manage to get hold of the telephone flex and pull the instrument to her. 'One day I said to Madame Marchand, who also lives by herself, "Luckily there is always the telephone." And she said to me, "But you still have to be able to get to it." ' In a most significant voice Maman repeated the last words several times: she added, 'If I had not managed to get there, I should have been done for.'

Would she have been able to shout loud enough to make herself heard? No, surely not. I pictured her distress. She believed in heaven, but in spite of her age, her feebleness, and her poor health, she clung ferociously to this world, and she had an animal dread of death. She had told my sister of a nightmare that she often had. 'I am being chased: I run, I run, and I come up against a wall; I have to jump over this wall, and I do not know what there is behind it; it terrifies me.' She also said to her, 'Death itself does not frighten me; it is the jump I am afraid of.' When she was creeping along the floor, she thought that the moment for the jump had come.

'It must have hurt dreadfully when you fell?' I asked her.

'No. I don't remember that it did. I didn't even feel it.'

So she lost consciousness, I thought. She remembered having felt giddy; she added that a few days before, when she had just taken one of her new medicines, she felt her legs giving way under her: she had just had time to lie down on her divan. I looked distrustfully at the bottles she had asked our young cousin Marthe Cordonnier to bring from her flat, together with various other things. She was bent on continuing the treatment: was this advisable?

Professor B came to see her at the end of the day and I followed him into the corridor. Once she had recovered, he said, my mother would walk no worse than before. 'She will be able to potter around again.' Did he think she had had a fainting-fit? Not at all. He seemed disconcerted when I told him that her bowels had been giving her trouble. The Boucicaut had reported a broken neck of the femur and he had confined himself to that: he would have her examined by a physician.

'You will be able to walk just as you did before,' I said to Maman. 'You will be able to go back to a normal life.'

'Oh, I shall never set foot in that flat again! I never want to see it any more. Not at any price!'

And she had been so proud of that flat. She had come to loathe the one in the rue de Rennes, which my father had filled with the noise of his ill-temper as he grew older and hypochondriac. After his death and my grandmother's, which happened very shortly after, she had wanted to make a break with her memories. Some years earlier a woman she knew had done up a studio, and this modernity quite dazzled Maman. In 1942, of course, it was easy enough to find somewhere to live, and she was able to make her dream come true: she rented a studio with a gallery, in the rue Blomet. She sold the ebonized pearwood desk, the Henri II dining-room suite, the double bed and the grand piano; she kept the rest of the furniture and some of the old red carpet. She hung my sister's paintings on the walls. She put a divan in the bedroom. In those days she went up and down the inside staircase perfectly happily. I did not think the place really very cheerful: it was on the second floor and in spite of the big windows overhead there was not much light. The upstairs rooms—bedroom, kitchen, bathroom—were always dark, and it was there that Maman spent most of her day since the time every stair began to force a groan out of her. In the course of twenty years everything, the walls, the furniture, the carpet, had grown worn and dirty. When the building changed hands in 1960 and Maman imagined she was going to be evicted she thought of a rest-home. She did not find anything she liked; and besides she was fond of her own place. She learnt that no one had the right to put her out and she stayed on in the rue Blomet. But now we—her friends and I—were going to look for a pleasant rest-home where she should settle as soon as she was better. 'You shall never go back to the rue Blomet, I promise you,' I said.

On Sunday her eyes were still half-closed; her memory was drowsing, and the words came drooping heavily from her lips. She told me about her 'calvary' again. Yet there was one thing that comforted her—the fact that they had brought her to this clinic: she had an ex-

aggerated notion of its excellence. 'At the Boucicaut they would have operated on me yesterday! It appears that *this* is the best clinic
in Paris.' And since for her the pleasure of prais-
ing was incomplete unless it was accompanied
by blame she added, referring to a nearby estab-
lishment, 'This is far better than the G Clinic.
I have been told that the G Clinic is not at all
the thing!'

'I have not slept so well for ages,' she said to
me on Monday. She had her normal look again;
her voice was clear and her eyes were taking
notice of the things around her. 'Dr Lacroix
ought to be sent some flowers.' I promised to
see to it. 'And what about the policemen?
Shouldn't they be given something? I put them
to great trouble.' I found it hard to convince
her that it was not called for.

She leaned back against her pillows, looked
straight at me and said very firmly, 'I have been
overdoing it, you know. I tired myself out—I
was at the end of my tether. I would not admit
that I was old. But one must face up to things:
in a few days I shall be seventy-eight, and that
is a great age. I must arrange my life accord-
ingly. I am going to start a fresh chapter.'

I gazed at her with admiration. For a great
while she had insisted upon considering herself
young. Once, when her son-in-law made a
clumsy remark, she had crossly replied, 'I know
very well that I am old, and I don't like it at
all: I don't care to be reminded of it.' Suddenly,
coming out of the fog she had been floating in
these three days past, she found the strength
to face her seventy-eight years, clear-sighted

and determined. 'I am going to start a fresh chapter.'

She had started a fresh chapter with astonishing courage after my father's death. It had grieved her very deeply indeed. But she had not bogged down in her past. She had taken advantage of the freedom that had been given back to her to rebuild a kind of life for herself that matched her own tastes. My father did not leave her a penny, and she was fifty-four. She passed examinations, attended courses, and won a certificate that enabled her to work as an assistant librarian in the Red Cross. She learnt to ride a bicycle again to go to her office. She thought of doing dress-making at home after the war. When that time came I was in a position to help her. But idleness did not suit her. She was eager to live in her own way at last and she discovered a whole mass of activities for herself. She looked after the library in an observation sanatorium just outside Paris as a volunteer, and then the one that belonged to a Catholic club in her neighborhood. She liked handling books, putting wrappers on them, arranging them, dealing with the tickets. giving advice to readers. She studied German and Italian, and kept up her English. She did embroidery at Dorcas meetings, took part in charity sales, attended lectures. She made herself a great many new friends: she also took up again with former acquaintances and relations whom my father's surliness had driven away, and she very cheerfully had them all to her studio. At last she was able to satisfy one of her oldest longings, and travel. She fought stubbornly against the anchylosis that was stiffening her legs. She went to see my sister in Vienna and Milan. In the summer she tripped through the streets of Florence and Rome. She went to see the museums of Belgium and Holland. During these last years, when she was almost paralysed, she gave up hurrying about the face of the earth. But when friends or cousins invited her out of Paris or into the country, nothing would stop her: she would have herself hoisted into the train by the guard without a second thought. Her greatest delight was to travel by car. A little while before, her great-niece Catherine had taken her to Meyrignac, driving by night in the little very slow Citroën—close on three hundred miles. She stepped out of the car as fresh as a blossom.

Her vitality filled me with wonder, and I respected her courage. Why, as soon as she could speak again, did she utter words that froze me? Telling me of her night at the Boucicaut she said, 'You know what the women of the lower classes are like: they moan.' 'These hospital nurses, they are only there for the money. So . . .' They were ready-made phrases, as automatic as drawing breath; but it was still her consciousness that gave them life and it was impossible to hear them without distress. The contrast between the truth of her suffering body and the nonsense that her head was stuffed with saddened me.

The physiotherapist came to Maman's bed, turned down the sheet and took hold of her left leg: Maman had an open hospital nightdress on and she did not mind that her wrinkled belly, criss-crossed with tiny lines, and her bald pubis showed. 'I no longer have any sort of shame,' she observed in a surprised voice.

'You are perfectly right not to have any,' I said. But I turned away and gazed fixedly into the garden. The sight of my mother's nakedness had jarred me. No body existed less for me: none existed more. As a child I had loved it dearly; as an adolescent it had filled me with an uneasy repulsion: all this was perfectly in the ordinary course of things and it seemed reasonable to me that her body should retain its dual nature, that it should be both repugnant and holy—a taboo. But for all that, I was astonished at the violence of my distress. My mother's indifferent acquiescence made it worse: she was abandoning the exigencies and prohibitions that had oppressed her all her life long and I approved of her doing so. Only this body, suddenly reduced by her capitulation to being a body and nothing more, hardly differed at all from a corpse—a poor defenceless carcass turned and manipulated by professional hands, one in which life seemed to carry on only because of its own stupid momentum. For me, my mother had always been there, and I had never seriously thought that some day, that soon I should see her go. Her death, like her birth, had its place in some legendary time. When I said to myself 'She is of an age to die' the words were devoid of meaning, as so many words are. For the first time I saw her as a dead body under suspended sentence.

The next morning I went to buy the night-dresses that the nurses had asked for—short ones, otherwise they wrinkled under the patient's bottom, which caused bed-sores.

'Do you want shorties? Baby-doll nighties?' asked the shop-assistants. I fingered frothy night-things as nonsensical as their names, in pastel colours, made for young, happy bodies. It was a lovely autumn day with a blue sky: I made my way through a lead-coloured world, and I realized that my mother's accident was affecting me far more than I had thought it would. I could not really see why. It had wrenched her out of the framework, the role, the set of images in which I had imprisoned her: I recognized her in this patient in bed, but I did not recognize either the pity or the kind of disturbance that she aroused in me. Finally I decided upon some pink three-quarter nightgowns with white spots.

Dr T, who was looking after Maman's general condition, came to see her while I was there.

'It seems that you eat too little?'

'I was depressed this summer. I didn't have the heart to eat.'

'You found cooking a nuisance?'

'What happened was that I made myself little treats, and then I left them.'

'Aha. It wasn't laziness, then. So you made yourself little treats?'

Maman concentrated. 'Once I made myself a cheese soufflé: after two spoonfuls I couldn't eat any more.'

'I see,' said Dr T, with a condescending smile.

Dr J, Professor B, Dr T: neat, trim, shining, well-groomed, bending over this ill-kempt, rather wild-looking old woman from an immense height: great men; bigwigs. I recognized that piddling self-importance: it was that of the judges on the bench when they have a man whose life is at stake before them. 'So you made yourself little treats?' There was no reason to smile while Maman was searching her memory with trustful willingness: it was her health that was at stake. And what right had B to say to me 'She will be able to potter around again'? I objected to his scale of values. I bristled when the privileged classes spoke through my mother's mouth; but I felt wholly on the side of the bedfast invalid struggling to thrust back paralysis and death.

On the other hand I did like the nurses; they were linked to their patient by the extreme closeness of those necessary tasks that were humiliating for her and revolting for them, and the interest they took in Maman did at least have the appearance of friendship. Mlle Laurent, the physiotherapist, could raise her spirits, give her a sense of security and calm her; and she never assumed any superiority.

'We will have your stomach X-rayed tomorrow,' said Dr T, finally.

Maman was distressed. 'So you are going to make me swallow that horrible stuff.'

'It's not as bad as all that!'

'Oh, but it is.' When she was alone with me she said pitifully, 'I can't tell you how nasty it is. It tastes vile.'

'Don't think about it in advance.'

But she could not think about anything else. Ever since she had entered the nursing-home the food had been her chief preoccupation.

Still, her childish concern surprised me. She had borne a great deal of sickness and pain without wincing. Was there a deeper anxiety hiding behind the fear of an unpleasant preparation? I did not ask myself that at the time.

The next day they told me that the X-rays—stomach and lungs—had gone off very well, and that there was nothing out of order. Maman, looking calm, wearing one of the pink nightgowns with white spots and the bed-jacket Olga had lent her, and with her hair in a big plait, no longer had the look of a sick woman. The use of her left arm had come back to her; she could unfold a paper, open a book or pick up the telephone without help. Wednesday. Thursday. Friday. Saturday. She did crosswords, read a book on Voltaire in love and Jean de Léry's account of his expedition in Brazil; she looked through *Le Figaro* and *France-Soir*. I came every morning; I only stayed an hour or two; she did not want to keep me any longer.. She had a great many visitors and sometimes indeed she complained of it: 'I have seen too many people today.' The room was full of flowers—cyclamens, azaleas, roses, anemones; and on her bedside table there were piles of boxes of chocolates and sweets.

'Don't you get bored?' I asked her.

'Oh, no!'

She was discovering the pleasures of being waited on, looked after, petted. Before, she had had to make a great effort to climb over the edge of her bath, helping herself with a stool; putting on her stockings had meant painful contortions. Now, a nurse came every morning and evening, and rubbed her with eau de Cologne and powdered her with talcum. Her meals were brought on a tray. 'There is one nurse who irritates me,' she said. 'She asks me when I expect to leave. But I don't want to leave at all.' When she was told that presently she would be able to sit up in an armchair and that presently she would be transferred to a convalescent home, her face clouded over: 'They are going to hustle me and push me about.' Yet there were times when she concerned herself with her future. A friend had talked to her about rest-homes an hour from Paris: 'No one will come and see me; I shall be too lonely,' she said unhappily. I assured her that she would not have to go into exile and I showed her the list of addresses I had gathered. She was quite happy to think of herself reading or knitting in the sun in the garden of a home at Neuilly. A little regretfully, but not without irony, she said, 'The people in my quarter are going to be sorry not to see me any more. The women at the club will miss me.' Once she said to me, 'I have lived for others too much. Now I shall become one of those self-centred old women who only live for themselves.' One thing worried her. 'I shan't be able to wash and dress myself any more.' I set her mind at rest: an attendant, a nurse, would look after that. Meanwhile, she was happily taking her ease in one of the beds of 'the best nursing-home in Paris, so much better than the G Clinic'. They paid the closest attention to her. As well as the X-rays there had been several blood-tests—everything was normal. Her temperature rose in the evening and I would have liked to know why; but the nurse did not seem to think it at all significant.

'I saw too many people yesterday, and they tired me,' she told me on Sunday. She was in a bad mood. Her usual nurses were off duty; an inexperienced girl had upset the bed-pan full of urine; the bed and even the bolster had been soaked. She closed her eyes often, and her recollection was confused. Dr T could not make out the plates that Dr D had sent and the next day there was to be a fresh intestinal X-ray. 'They will give me a barium enema, and it hurts,' Maman told me. 'And they are going to shake me about again and trundle me around: I should so like to be left in peace.'

I pressed her damp, rather cold hand. 'Don't think about it in advance. Don't worry. Worrying is bad for you.'

Gradually her spirits came back, but she seemed weaker than the day before. Friends telephoned and I answered. 'Well!' I said to her, 'There is no end to it. The Queen of England wouldn't be more spoilt—flowers, letters, sweeties, telephone-calls! What quantities of people think of you!' I was holding her tired hand: she kept her eyes shut, but there was a faint smile on her sad mouth. 'They like me because I am cheerful.'

She expected many visitors on Monday and I was busy. I did not come until Tuesday morning. I opened the door and stopped dead. Maman, who was so thin, seemed to have grown still thinner and more shrivelled, wizened, dried up, a pinkish twig. In a somewhat bewildered voice she whispered, 'They have dried me out completely.' She had waited until the evening to be X-rayed and for twenty hours on end they had not allowed her to drink. The barium enema had not hurt; but the thirst and the anxiety had quite worn her out. Her face had dissolved: she was tense with unhappiness. What was the result of the X-rays? 'We can't understand them,' the nurses replied in frightened voices. I managed to see Dr T. The information the plates gave was still obscure: according to him there was no 'pocket', but the bowel was contorted by spasms, nervous in origin, which had prevented it from working since the day before. My mother was obstinately sanguine; but for all that she was anxious and highly-strung—that was the explanation of her tics. She was too exhausted to see visitors and she asked me to telephone Father P, her confessor, and put him off. She scarcely spoke to me, and she could not manage a smile.

'I'll see you tomorrow evening,' I said as I left. My sister was arriving during the night and she would go to the clinic in the morning. At nine in the evening my telephone rang. It was Professor B. 'I should like to have a night-nurse for your mother: do you agree? She is not well. You thought of not coming until tomorrow evening: it would be better to be there in the morning.' In the end he told me that there was a tumour blocking the small intestine: Maman had cancer.

Cancer. It was all about us. Indeed, it was

patently obvious—those ringed eyes, that thinness. But her doctor had ruled out that hypothesis. And it is notorious that the parents are the last to admit that their son is mad; the children that their mother has cancer. We believed it all the less since that was what she had been afraid of all her life. When she was forty, if she knocked her chest against a piece of furniture she grew terribly frightened—'I shall have cancer of the breast.' Last winter one of my friends had been operated upon for cancer of the stomach. 'That is what is going to happen to me, too.' I had shrugged: there is a very wide difference between cancer and a sluggishness of the bowels that is treated with tamarind jelly. We never imagined that Maman's obsession could possibly be justified. Yet—she told us this later—it was cancer that Francine Diato thought of: 'I recognized that expression. And,' she added, 'that smell, too.' Everything became clear. Maman's sudden illness in Alsace arose from her tumour. The tumour had caused her fainting-fit and her fall. And these two weeks of bed had brought on the blockage of the intestine that had been threatening for a long while.

Poupette, who had telephoned Maman several times, thought she was in excellent health. Poupette was closer to her than I: she was fonder of her, too. I could not let her come to the nursing-home and all at once see death on her face. I telephoned her at the Diatos', a little while after her train had got in. She was already asleep: what an awakening!

On that Wednesday, 6 November, the gas, the electricity and public transport were on strike. I had asked Bost to come and fetch me by car. Before he arrived Professor B telephoned again: Maman had vomited all night long; in all likelihood she would not get through the day.

The streets were less blocked with traffic than I had feared. At about ten I met Poupette outside the door of room 114. I repeated what Professor B had said. She told me that since the beginning of the morning a resuscitation expert, Dr N, had been working on Maman: he was going to put a tube into her nose to clean out her stomach. 'But what's the good of tormenting her, if she is dying? Let her die in peace,' said Poupette, in tears. I sent her down to Bost, who was waiting in the hall: he would take her to have some coffee. Dr N passed by me; I stopped him. White coat, white cap: a young man with an unresponsive face. 'Why this tube? Why torture Maman, since there's no hope?' He gave me a withering look. 'I am doing what has to be done.' He opened the door. After a moment a nurse told me to come in.

The bed was back in its ordinary place in the middle of the room with its head against the wall. On the left there was an intravenous dripper, connected with Maman's arm. From her nose there emerged a tube of transparent plastic that passed through some complicated apparatus and ended in a jar. Her nose was pinched and her face had shrunk even more:

it had the saddest air of submission. In a whisper
she told me that the tube did not worry her
too much, but that during the night she had
suffered a great deal. She was thirsty and she
was not allowed to drink: the nurse put a thin
tube to her mouth with the other end in a glass
of water; Maman moistened her lips, without
swallowing. I was fascinated by the sucking
motion, at once avid and restrained, of her lip,
with its faint downy shadow, that rounded just
as it had rounded in my childhood whenever
Maman was cross or embarrassed. 'Would you
like me to have left that in her stomach?' said
N aggressively, showing me the jar full of a
yellowish substance. I did not reply. In the
corridor he said 'At dawn she had scarcely four
hours left. I have brought her back to life.' I did
not venture to ask him 'For what?'

Consultation of specialists. My sister at my
side while a physician and a surgeon, Dr P,
palpate the swollen abdomen. Maman groans
under their fingers: she cries out. Morphine
injection. She still groans. 'Another injection,'
we beg. They are against it: too much morphine
would paralyse the intestine. What are they
hoping for then? There is no electricity, because
of the strike, and they have sent a blood-sample
to the American hospital, which has its own
generator. Are they thinking of operating? That
is hardly possible, the surgeon tells me as he
leaves the room; the patient is too weak. He
walks away, and an elderly nurse, Mme Gontrand, who has heard him, bursts out, 'Don't let
her be operated on!' Then she claps her hand

to her mouth. 'If Dr N knew I had said that to you! I was speaking as if it were my own mother.' I question her. 'What will happen if they do operate on her?' But she has closed up again: she does not answer.

Maman had gone to sleep: I went away, leaving telephone numbers with Poupette. When she called me at Sartre's place at about five there was hope in her voice. 'The surgeon wants to try the operation. The blood analyses are very encouraging; her strength has come back, and her heart will stand it. And after all, it is not absolutely sure that it is cancer: perhaps it is just peritonitis. If it is, she has a chance. Do you agree?'

Don't let them operate on her.

'Yes, I agree. When?'

'Be here by two. They will not tell her they are going to operate; they will say they are going to X-ray her again.'

'Don't let them operate on her.' A frail argument against the decision of a specialist; a frail argument against my sister's hopes. Maman might not wake up again? That was not the worst way out. And I did not imagine that a surgeon would take that risk: she would get over it. Would the operation hasten the development of the disease? No doubt that is what Mme Gontrand had meant. But with the intestinal obstruction at this stage Maman could not survive three days, and I was terribly afraid that her death might be appalling.

An hour later the telephone, and Poupette sobbing, 'Come at once. They have operated:

they found a huge cancerous tumour. . .' Sartre
went down with me; he took me in a taxi as far
as the nursing-home. My throat was constricted
with anguish. A male nurse showed me the
lobby between the entrance-hall and the operating-theatre where my sister was waiting. She
was so upset that I asked for a tranquillizer for
her. She told me that the doctors had warned
Maman, in a very natural voice, that before
X-raying her they would give her a sedative
injection; Dr N had put her to sleep; Poupette
had held Maman's hand right through the
anaesthetizing, and I could imagine what a trial
it had been for her, the sight of that old, ravaged body, quite naked—that body which was
her mother's. Maman's eyes had turned up; her
mouth had opened: Poupette would never be
able to forget that face, either. They had
wheeled her into the operating-theatre and Dr
N had come out a moment later: four pints
of pus in the abdomen, the peritoneum burst,
a huge tumour, a cancer of the worst kind.
The surgeon was removing everything that
could be removed. While we were there, waiting, my cousin Jeanne came in with her daughter Chantal; she had just come from Limoges
and she thought she would find Maman quietly
in bed: Chantal had brought a book of crossword puzzles. We discussed what we should
say to Maman when she woke up. It was easy
enough: the X-ray had shown that she had
peritonitis and an operation had been decided
upon at once.

Maman had just been taken up to her room,

N told us. He was triumphant: she had been half-dead that morning and yet she had withstood a long and serious operation excellently. Thanks to the very latest methods of anaesthesia her heart, lungs, the whole organism had continued to function normally. There was no sort of doubt that he entirely washed his hands of the consequences of that feat. My sister had said to the surgeon, 'Operate on Maman. But if it is cancer, promise me that you will not let her suffer.' He had promised. What was his word worth?

Maman was sleeping, lying flat on her back, her face the colour of wax, her nose pinched, her mouth open. My sister and a night-nurse would sit up with her. I went home; I talked to Sartre; we played some Bartók. Suddenly, at eleven, an outburst of tears that almost degenerated into hysteria.

Amazement. When my father died I did not cry at all. I had said to my sister, 'It will be the same for Maman.' I had understood all my sorrows up until that night: even when they flowed over my head I recognized myself in them. This time my despair escaped from my control: someone other than myself was weeping in me. I talked to Sartre about my mother's mouth as I had seen it that morning and about everything I had interpreted in it—greediness refused, an almost servile humility, hope, distress, loneliness—the loneliness of her death and of her life—that did not want to admit its existence. And he told me that my own mouth was not obeying me any more: I had put Maman's mouth on my own face and in spite of myself, I copied its movements. Her whole person, her whole being, was concentrated there, and compassion wrung my heart.

I DO NOT think my mother can have been a happy child. I only remember her speaking of one pleasant memory—her grandmother's garden in a village in Lorraine, and the little plums and greengages they ate, warm from the tree. She never told me anything about her childhood at Verdun. There is a photograph of her, aged eight and dressed as a daisy. 'You had a pretty costume,' I said. 'Yes,' she answered, 'but the dye came out of my green stockings and worked deep into my skin. It took three days to get rid of it.' Her voice was sullen: a past full of bitterness was running through her mind. She complained to me more than once of her mother's coldness. When my grandmother was fifty she was detached and even haughty, a woman who laughed little, gossiped much, and showed no more than a conventional affection for Maman: she was fanatically devoted to her husband, and her children had only a secondary place in her life. Speaking to me of my grandfather, Maman often said resentfully, 'He never had time for anyone but your Aunt Lili.' Lili, five years younger, pink and fair, aroused a fervent, ineradicable jealousy in her sister. Until

I began to reach adolescence Maman ascribed to me the loftiest intellectual and moral qualities: she identified herself with me and she humiliated and slighted my sister—Poupette was the younger sister, pink and fair, and without realizing it, Maman was taking her revenge upon her.

She told me proudly about Les Oiseaux and the Mother Superior, whose good opinion had consoled her self-esteem. She showed me a photograph of her class: six girls sitting in a park between two nuns. There are four boarders, dressed in black, and two day-girls, in white frocks—Maman and one of her friends. They are all wearing high tuckers, long skirts, severe buns. There is no expression whatever in their eyes. Maman started life corseted in the most rigid of principles—provincial propriety and the morals of a convent-girl.

When she was twenty she suffered another emotional set-back: the cousin she had fallen in love with preferred another girl, also a cousin, my Aunt Germaine. All her life long she retained an underlying sensitivity and rancour arising from these disappointments.

When she was with my father she came into flower. She loved him, she admired him, and there is not the slightest doubt that for ten years he made her entirely happy physically. He loved women; he had had many affairs; and like Marcel Prévost, whom he read with delight, he thought that a young wife ought not to be treated with less ardour than a mistress. Maman's face, with that faint down on her upper lip, betrayed a warm voluptuousness.

The understanding between them was perfectly apparent: he stroked her arm, petted her, whispered affectionate nonsense. I see her again as I saw her one morning—I was six or seven—barefoot on the red carpet of the corridor in her long white linen nightgown; her hair fell in a twist on the back of her neck and I was struck by the radiance of her smile, which, for me, was associated in some mysterious way with that bedroom she had just left; I scarcely recognized this brilliant vision as the respectable grown-up who was my mother.

But nothing, ever, wipes out childhood. And Maman's happiness was not unalloyed. My father's selfishness burst out as early as their honeymoon: she wanted to see the Italian Lakes; they went no further than Nice, where the racing season had just begun. She often recalled this disappointment, not with any grudge, but not without regret. She loved travelling. 'I should have liked to be an explorer,' she used to say. The happiest times of her young days were those excursions on bicycle or on foot, through the Vosges or Luxembourg, which my grandfather organized. She had to give up many of the things she had dreamt of: my father's wishes always came before hers. She stopped seeing her old friends, whose husbands he found boring. He only enjoyed himself in drawing-rooms or on the stage. She cheerfully followed him there: she liked social events. But her beauty did not protect her from spitefulness: she was provincial and not very quickwitted; people smiled at her awkwardness in that very Parisian society. Some of the women

she met there had had affairs with my father:
I can imagine whisperings, betrayals. In his
desk my father kept the photograph of his last
mistress, a pretty, brilliant woman who sometimes came to the house with her husband.
Thirty years later he said to Maman, laughing,
'You did away with her photo.' She denied it,
but he was not convinced. One thing is sure,
and that is that even at the time of her honeymoon she suffered both in her love and her
pride. She was passionate and headstrong: her
wounds healed slowly.

And then my grandfather went bankrupt. She
thought herself dishonoured, so much so that
she broke with all her connexions at Verdun.
The dowry promised to my father was not paid.
She thought it extremely noble in him not to
blame her, and she felt guilty towards him all
her life.

But for all that, a successful marriage, two
daughters who loved her dearly, some degree
of affluence—until the end of the war Maman
did not complain of her fate. She was affectionate, she was gay, and her smile ravished
my heart.

When my father's circumstances changed
and we experienced semi-poverty, Maman decided to look after the house without a servant.
Unfortunately, housework bored her terribly,
and she thought she was lowering herself by
doing it. She was capable of selfless devotion
for my father and for us. But it is impossible
for anyone to say 'I am sacrificing myself' without feeling bitterness. One of Maman's contradictions was that she thoroughly believed in

the nobility of devotion, while at the same time she had tastes, aversions and desires that were too masterful for her not to loathe whatever went against them. She was continually rebelling against the restraints and the privations that she inflicted upon herself.

It is a pity that out-of-date ideas should have prevented her from adopting the solution that she came round to, twenty years later—that of working away from home. She had a good memory, she was persevering and conscientious; she might have become a secretary or have worked in a book-shop: she would have risen in her own esteem instead of feeling that she was losing caste. She would have had connexions of her own. She would have escaped from a state of dependence that tradition made her think natural but that did not in the least agree with her nature. And no doubt she would then have been better equipped to bear the frustration that she had to put up with.

I do not blame my father. It is tolerably well known that in men habit kills desire. Maman had lost her first freshness and he his ardour. In order to arouse it he turned to the professionals of the café de Versailles, or the young ladies of the Sphinx. More than once, between the age of fifteen and twenty, I saw him coming home at eight in the morning, smelling of drink, and telling confused tales of bridge or poker. Maman made no scenes: perhaps she believed him, so trained was she at running away from awkward truths. But she could not happily adapt herself to his indifference. Her case alone would be enough to convince me that bourgeois marriage is an unnatural institution. The wedding-ring on her finger had authorized her to become acquainted with pleasure; her senses had grown demanding; at thirty-five, in the prime of her life, she was no longer allowed to satisfy them. She went on sleeping beside the man whom she loved, and who almost never made love to her any more: she hoped, she waited and she pined, in vain. Complete abstinence would have been less of a trial for her pride than this promiscuity. I am not surprised that her temper should have deteriorated: slaps, nagging, scenes, not only in privacy, but even when guests were there. 'Françoise has a disgusting character,' my father used to say. She admitted that she 'flew off the handle' easily. But she was bitterly hurt when she heard that people said 'Françoise is so pessimistic!' or 'Françoise is becoming neurotic.'

When she was a young woman she loved clothes. Her face would light up when people told her that she looked like my elder sister. One of my father's cousins, who played the 'cello and whom she accompanied on the piano, paid her respectful attentions: when he married she loathed his wife. When her sexual and her social life dwindled away Maman stopped taking care of her appearance, except on grand occasions when 'dressing up' was essential. I remember coming back from the holidays once: she met us at the station, and she was wearing a pretty velvet hat with a little veil, and she had put on some powder. My sister was delighted and she cried, 'Maman, you look just like a fashionable lady!' She laughed unreservedly, for she no longer prided herself on elegance. Both for her daughters and for herself, she pushed the contempt for the body that she had been taught at the convent to the point of uncleanliness. Yet—and this was another of her contradictions—she still retained the desire to please; flatteries flattered her; she replied to them coquettishly. She was filled with pride when one of my father's friends dedicated a book (published at the author's expense) to her— *To Françoise de Beauvoir, whose life I so admire.* An ambiguous tribute: she earned admiration by a self-effacement that deprived her of admirers.

Cut off from the pleasures of the body, deprived of the satisfactions of vanity, tied down to wearisome tasks that bored and humiliated her, this proud and obstinate woman did not possess the gift of resignation. Between her fits of anger she was perpetually singing, gossiping, making jokes, drowning her heart's complaints with noise. When, after my father's death, Aunt Germaine hinted that he had not been an ideal husband, Maman snubbed her fiercely. 'He always made me very happy.' And certainly that was what she always told herself. Still, this forced optimism was not enough to satisfy her hunger. She flung herself into the only other course that was available to her—that of feeding upon the young lives that were in her care. 'At least I have never been self-centred; I have lived for others,' she said to me later. Yes, but also by means of others. She was possessive; she was overbearing; she would have liked to have us completely in her power. But it was just at the time when this compensation became necessary to her that we began to long for freedom and solitude. Conflicts worked themselves up and broke out; and they were no help to Maman in recovering her balance.

Yet she was the strongest: it was her will that won. At home we had to leave all the doors open, and I had to work under her eye, in the room where she was sitting. When, at night, my sister and I chattered from one bed to the other, she pressed her ear against the wall, eaten up with curiosity, and called out, 'Be quiet!' She would not let us learn to swim, and she prevented my father from buying us bicycles: we would have escaped from her through these pleasures that she could not have shared. She insisted upon taking part in all our amusements, and this was not only because she had few of her own: for reasons that no doubt went back to her childhood, she could not bear to feel left out. She did not scruple to force herself upon us, even when she knew she was not wanted. One night at La Grillère, we were in the kitchen with a whole band of friends of our cousins, boys and girls: we were cooking the crayfish that we had just caught by the light of lanterns. Maman burst in, the only grown-up: 'I certainly have the right to have supper with you.' She cast a great damp on everything, but she stayed. Later, my cousin Jacques and my sister and I had agreed to meet at the door of the Salon d'Automne; Maman went with us; he did not appear. 'I saw your mother, so I went away,' he said the next day. She always made her presence felt. When we invited friends to the house—'I certainly have the right to have tea with you'—she monopolized the conversation. At Vienna and Milan my sister was often dismayed by the confidence with which Maman thrust herself forward during more or less official dinners.

These heavy-handed intrusions, these outbursts of self-consequence, were opportunities for getting her own back: she did not often have the chance of asserting herself. She had few social contacts, and when my father was there it was he who held the stage. The expression that we found so vexing, 'I certainly have the right', in fact proves her want of self-assurance; her desires did not carry their own justification with them. She had no self-control and at times she was a shrew; but ordinarily she pushed discretion to the point of humility. She quarrelled with my father over trifles, but she never ventured to ask him for money; she spent none on herself and as little as possible on us; meekly she let him spend all his evenings away from home and go out by himself on Sundays. After his death, when she was dependent on Poupette and me, she had the same scruple with regard to us, the same desire not to be a nuisance. She was under an obligation to us and she no longer had any other way of showing us her feelings; whereas formerly in her eyes the trouble she took over us justified her tyranny.

Her love for us was deep as well as exclusive, and the pain it caused us as we submitted to it was a reflection of her own conflicts. She was very open to wounds—she was capable of chewing over a reproof or a criticism for thirty or forty years—and her diffused indwelling resentment made itself apparent in aggressive forms of behaviour—brutal frankness, heavily ironic remarks. With regard to us, she often displayed a cruel unkindness that was more thoughtless than sadistic: her desire was not to cause us unhappiness but to prove her own power to herself. When I was spending my holidays with Zaza, my sister wrote to me: an adolescent girl, she told me about her heart, her soul, her problems; I replied. Maman opened my letter and read it aloud in front of Poupette, shrieking with laughter at its confidences. Poupette, stiff with fury, overwhelmed her with her scorn and swore that she would never forgive her. Maman burst into tears and begged me, in a letter, to bring them together again: which I did.

She wanted to make sure of her power over my sister above all, and she grew jealous of our friendship. When she knew that I had lost my faith she said very loudly and angrily to Poupette, 'I shall defend you against her influence. I shall protect you!' During the holidays she forbade us to see one another alone: we met secretly in the chestnut woods. This jealousy tormented her all her life, and until the end we still kept the habit of hiding most of our meetings from her.

But it also often happened that we were moved by the warmth of her affection. When Poupette was about seventeen she was the involuntary cause of a quarrel between Papa and 'Uncle' Adrien, whom he considered his best friend: Maman defended her fiercely against my father, who would not speak to his daughter for months. Later on he held it against my sister that she would not sacrifice her vocation as a painter in order to earn her bread and butter, and that she went on living at home: he would not give her a penny and he barely fed her. Maman stood up for her and used all her ingenuity to help her. For my part, I have not forgotten how sweetly, after my father's death, she urged me to go off on a journey with a friend, when a single sigh from her would have kept me back.

She spoilt her relationships with other people by clumsiness: nothing could have been more pitiful than her attempts at separating my sister and me. When our cousin Jacques— she transferred to him a little of the love she had had for his father—took to coming to the rue de Rennes less frequently she received him every time with little scenes that she thought amusing and that he found irritating: he came less and less often. There were tears in her eyes when I settled in Grandmama's house, and I was grateful to her for not making even the first hint of an emotional display— that was something she always avoided. Yet every time I had dinner at home that year she grumbled that I was neglecting my family, although in fact I came very often. She would not ask for anything, out of pride and upon principle; and then she complained of not being given enough.

She could not discuss her difficulties with anyone at all, not even herself. She had not been taught to see her own motives plainly nor to use her own judgment. She had to take shelter behind authority: but the authorities she respected were not in agreement; there was hardly a single point in common between the Mother Superior of Les Oiseaux and my father. I had experienced this setting of one idea against another while my mind was being formed and not after it was set: thanks to my early childhood I had a confidence in myself that my mother did not possess in the least: the road of argument, disputation—my road— was closed to her. On the contrary, she had made up her mind to share the general opinion: the last person who spoke to her was right. She read a great deal; but although she had an excellent memory she forgot almost everything. Exact knowledge, a decided view, would have made the sudden reversals that circumstances might force upon her impossible. Even after my father's death she retained this prudent attitude. The people she then mixed with were more of her way of thinking. She sided with the 'enlightened' Catholics against the integrists. Yet the people she knew differed on many points. And on the other hand, although I was living in sin, my opinion counted in many things, and so did those of my sister and Lionel. She dreaded 'looking a fool' in our eyes. So she remained woolly-minded and she went on saying yes to everything and being surprised by nothing. In her last years she did attain some kind of coherence in her ideas, but at the time when her emotional life was at its most tormented she possessed no doctrine, no concepts, no words with which to rationalize her situation. That was the source of her bewildered uneasiness.

Thinking against oneself often bears fruit; but with my mother it was another question again—she *lived* against herself. She had appetites in plenty: she spent all her strength in repressing them and she underwent this denial in anger. In her childhood her body, her heart and her mind had been squeezed into an armour of principles and prohibitions. She had been taught to pull the laces hard and tight herself. A full-blooded, spirited woman lived on inside her, but a stranger to herself, deformed and mutilated.

As soon as I woke up, I telephoned my sister. Maman had come to in the middle of the night; she knew that she had been operated upon and she hardly seemed at all surprised. I took a cab. The same journey, the same warm blue autumn, the same nursing-home. But I was stepping into another story: instead of a convalescence, a death-bed. Before, I came here to spend comparatively unemotional hours; I went through the hall without paying attention. It was behind those closed doors that the tragedies were taking place: nothing showed through. From now on one of these dramas belonged to me. I went up the stairs as quickly as I could, as slowly as I could. Now there was a sign hanging on the door: No Visitors. The scene had changed. The bed was in the position it had been the day before, with both sides free. The sweets had been put away in cupboards; so had the books. There were no flowers any more on the big table in the corner, but bottles, balloon-flasks, test-tubes. Maman was asleep: she no longer had the tube in her nose and it was less painful to look at her, but, under the bed, one could see jars and pipes that

communicated with her stomach and her intestines. Her left arm was attached to an intravenous drip. She was no longer wearing any
clothes whatever: the bed-jacket was spread
over her chest and her naked shoulders. A new
character had made her appearance—a private
nurse, Mademoiselle Leblon, as gracious as an
Ingres portrait. She had a blue headdress to
cover her hair and white padded slippers on
her feet: she supervised the drip and shook the
flask to dilute its plasma. My sister told me
that according to the doctors a respite of some
weeks or even of some months was not impossible. She had said to Professor B 'But what
shall we say to Maman when the disease starts
again, in another place?' 'Don't worry about
that. We shall find something to say. We always
do. And the patient always believes it.'

In the afternoon Maman had her eyes open:
she spoke so that one could hardly make out
what she said, but sensibly. 'Well,' I said to
her, 'so you break your leg and they go and
operate on you for appendicitis!'

She raised one finger and, with a certain
pride, whispered, 'Not appendicitis. Pe-ri-ton-
it-is.' She added. 'What luck . . . be here.'

'You are glad that I am here?'

'No. Me.' Peritonitis: and her being in this
clinic had saved her! The betrayal was beginning. 'Glad not to have that tube. So glad!'

With the removal of the filth that had swollen her abdomen the day before, she was no
longer in pain. And with her two daughters at
her bedside she believed that she was safe.
When Dr P and Dr N came in she said to them

in a contented voice, 'I am not forsaken,' before
she closed her eyes again. They spoke to one
another: 'It is extraordinary how quickly she
has picked up. Amazing!' Indeed it was. Thanks
to the transfusions and the infusions Maman's
face had some colour again and a look of health.
The poor suffering thing that had been lying
on this bed the day before had turned back into
a woman.

I showed Maman the book of crosswords
Chantal had brought. Speaking to the nurse she
faltered, 'I have a big dictionary, the new La-
rousse; I treated myself to it, for crosswords.'
That dictionary: one of her last delights. She
had talked to me about it for a long time before she bought it, and her face lit up every
time I consulted it. 'We'll bring it for you,'
I said.

'Yes. And *Le Nouvel Œdipe* too; I have not
got all the . . .'

One had to listen very intently to catch the
words that she laboured to breathe out; words
whose mystery made them as disturbing as
those of an oracle. Her memories, her desires,
her anxieties were floating somewhere outside
time, turned into unreal and poignant dreams
by her childlike voice and the imminence of
her death.

She slept a great deal; from time to time she
took up a few drops of water through the tube;
she spat in paper handkerchiefs that the nurse
held to her mouth. In the evening she began
to cough: Mademoiselle Laurent, who had come
to ask after her, straightened her up, massaged
her and helped her to spit. Afterwards Maman

looked at her with a real smile—the first for four days.

Poupette decided to spend her nights at the nursing-home. 'You were with Papa and Grandmama when they died; I was far away,' she said to me. 'I am going to look after Maman. Besides, I want to stay with her.'

I agreed. Maman was astonished. 'What do you want to sleep here for?'

'I slept in Lionel's room when he was operated on. It's always done.'

'Oh, I see.'

I went home, feverish with 'flu. Leaving the overheated clinic I had caught cold in the autumnal dampness: I went to bed, stupefied with pills. I did not switch off the telephone: Maman might die at any moment, 'blown out like a candle', said the doctors, and my sister was to call me at the least alarm. The bell woke me with a start: four in the morning. 'It is the end.' I picked up the receiver and heard an unknown voice: a wrong number. I could not get to sleep again until dawn. At half-past eight the telephone bell again: I ran for it— an utterly unimportant message. I loathed the hearse-black apparatus: 'Your mother has cancer. Your mother will not get through the night.' One of these days it would crackle into my ear, 'It is the end.'

I go through the garden. I go into the hall. You might think you were in an airport—low tables, modern armchairs, people kissing one another as they say hallo or good-bye, others waiting, suitcases, hold-alls, flowers in the vases, bouquets wrapped in shiny paper as if they were meant for welcoming travellers about to land . . . But there is a feeling of something not quite right in the whisperings, the expressions. And sometimes a man entirely clothed in white appears in the opening of the door at the far end, and there is blood on his shoes. I go up one floor. On my left a long corridor with the bedrooms, the nurses' rooms and the duty-room. On the right a square lobby furnished with an upholstered bench and a desk with a white telephone standing upon it. The one side gives on to a waiting-room; the other on to room 114. No Visitors. Beyond the door I come to a short passage: on the left the lavatory with the wash-stand, the bed-pan, cotton-wool, jars; on the right a cupboard which holds Maman's things; on a coat-hanger there is the red dressing-gown, all dusty. 'I never want to see that dressing-gown again.' I open the second door. Before, I went through all this without seeing it. Now I know that it will form part of my life for ever.

'I am very well,' said Maman. With a knowing air she added, 'When the doctors were talking to one another yesterday, I heard them. They said, "It's amazing!"' This word delighted her: she often pronounced it, gravely, as though it were a spell that guaranteed her recovery. Yet she still felt very weak and her overriding desire was to avoid the slightest effort. Her dream was to be fed by drip all her life long. 'I shall never eat again.'

'What, you who so loved your food?'

'No. I shall not eat any more.'

Mademoiselle Leblon took a brush and comb to do her hair for her: 'Cut it all off,' Maman ordered firmly. We protested. 'You will tire me: cut it off, do.' She insisted with a strange obstinacy: it was as though she wanted to bring lasting rest by making this sacrifice. Gently Mademoiselle Leblon undid her plait and untangled her hair; she plaited it again and pinned the silvery coil round Maman's head. Maman's relaxed face had recovered a surprising purity and I thought of a Leonardo drawing of a very beautiful old woman. 'You are as beautiful as a Leonardo,' I said.

She smiled. 'I was not so bad, once upon a time.' In a rather mysterious voice she told the nurse, 'I had lovely hair, and I did it up in bandeaux round my head.' And she went on talking about herself, how she had taken her librarian's diploma, her love for books. As Mademoiselle Leblon answered, she was preparing a flask of serum: she explained to me that the clear fluid also contained glucose and various salts. 'A positive cocktail,' I observed.

All day long we dazed Maman with plans. She listened, with her eyes closed. My sister and her husband had just bought an old farmhouse in Alsace and they were going to have it done up. Maman would have a big room, completely independent, and there she would finish her convalescence. 'But wouldn't it bore Lionel if I were to stay for a long while?'

'Of course not.'

'To be sure, I wouldn't be in the way there. At Scharrachbergen it was too small: I was a nuisance.'

We talked about Meyrignac. Maman went back to her memories of the time she was a young woman there. And for years past she had been enthusiastically telling me about the improvements at Meyrignac. She was very fond of Jeanne, whose three elder daughters lived in Paris and very often came to see her at the clinic—pretty, blooming, cheerful girls.

'I have no granddaughters and they have no grandmother,' she explained to Mademoiselle Leblon. 'So I am their grandmother.'

While she was dozing I looked at a paper: opening her eyes she asked me, 'What is happening at Saigon?' I told her the news. Once, in a tone of bantering reproof, she observed, 'I was operated on behind my back!' and when Dr P came in she said, 'Here is the guilty man,' but in a laughing voice. He stayed with her for a little while, and when he remarked, 'It is never too late to learn', she replied in a rather solemn tone, 'Yes. I have learnt that I had peritonitis.'

I said jokingly, 'You really are extraordinary! You come in to have your femur patched up, and they operate on you for peritonitis!'

'It's quite true. I am not an ordinary woman at all!'

This circumstance, this mistake, amused her for days. 'I tricked Professor B thoroughly. He thought he was going to operate on my leg, but in fact Dr P operated on me for peritonitis.'

What touched our hearts that day was the way she noticed the slightest agreeable sensation: it was as though, at the age of seventy-eight, she were waking afresh to the miracle of living. While the nurse was settling her pillows the metal of a tube touched her thigh—'It's cool!

How pleasant!' She breathed in the smell of eau de Cologne and talcum powder—'How good it smells.' She had the bunches of flowers and the plants arranged on her wheeled table. 'The little red roses come from Meyrignac. At Meyrignac there are roses still.' She asked us to raise the curtain that was covering the window and she looked at the golden leaves of the trees. 'How lovely. I shouldn't see that from my flat!' She smiled. And both of us, my sister and I, had the same thought: it was that same smile that had dazzled us when we were little children, the radiant smile of a young woman. Where had it been between then and now?

'If she has a few days of happiness like this, keeping her alive will have been worth while,' said Poupette to me. But what was it going to cost?

'This is a death-chamber,' I thought the next day. Across the window there was a heavy blue curtain. (The blind was broken and it could not be pulled down; but formerly the light had not worried Maman.) She was lying in the darkness with her eyes closed. I took her hand and she whispered, 'It's Simone: and I can't see you!' Poupette left; I opened a detective story. From time to time Maman sighed, 'I am not in my right mind.' To Dr P she complained, 'I am in a coma.'

'If you were, you wouldn't know it.'

That reply comforted her. A little later she said to me with a thoughtful air, 'I have undergone a very grave operation. I am a person who has been operated upon in a very serious way.' I improved on this and little by little she recovered her spirits. The evening before, she told me, she had dreamed with her eyes open. 'There were men in the room, evil men dressed in blue; they wanted to take me away and make me drink cocktails. Your sister sent them off . . .' I had said the word cocktail, talking about the mixture that Mademoiselle Leblon was getting ready; she was wearing a blue headdress; as for the men, they were the male nurses who had taken Maman off to the operating theatre. 'Yes. That's it, no doubt . . .' She asked me to open the window. 'How pleasant it is to have fresh air.' Birds were singing and she was enchanted. 'Birds!' And before I went away she said, 'It's odd. I feel a yellow light on my left cheek. A pretty light coming through a yellow paper: it's very pleasant.'

I asked Dr P, 'Has the operation in itself been a success?'

'It will have been a success if the movement through the intestines starts again. We shall know within two or three days.'

I liked Dr P. He did not assume consequential airs; he talked to Maman as though she were a human being and he answered my questions willingly. On the other hand, Dr N and I did not get along together at all. He was smart, athletic, energetic, infatuated with technique, and he had resuscitated Maman with great zeal; but for him she was the subject of an interesting experiment and not a person. He frightened us. Maman had an old relative who had been kept alive in a coma for the last six months. 'I hope you wouldn't let them keep me going like that,' she had said to us. 'It's horrible!' If Dr N took it into his head to beat a record he would be a dangerous opponent.

'He woke Maman to give her an enema that did not work,' Poupette told me in distress on Sunday morning. 'Why does he torment her?' I stopped N as he went by: he never spoke to me of his own accord. Once again I begged him, 'Do not torment her.' And in an outraged tone he replied, 'I am not tormenting her. I am doing what has to be done.'

The blue curtain was raised, the room less gloomy. Maman had had herself bought some dark glasses. She took them off as I came in. 'Ah, today I can see you!' She felt well in herself. In a calm voice she said, 'Tell me, have I a right side?'

'How do you mean? Of course you have.'

'It's funny: yesterday they told me that I looked well. But I only looked well on the left side. I felt the other was all grey. It seemed to me that I had no right side any more—that I was divided into two. Now it's coming back a little.'

I touched her right cheek. 'Do you feel that?'

'Yes, but as though it were a dream.'

I touched her left cheek.

'That's real,' she said.

The broken thigh, the operation-wound, the dressings, the tubes, the infusions—all that happened on the left side. Was that why the other no longer seemed to exist?

'You look splendid. The doctors are very pleased with you,' I asserted.

'No. Dr N is not pleased: he wants me to break wind for him.' She smiled to herself.

'When I get out of here I shall send him a box of those chocolate dog-messes.'

The pneumatic mattress massaged her skin; there were pads between her knees, and they had a hoop over them to prevent the sheets from touching; another arrangement stopped her heels touching the draw-sheet: but for all that, bed-sores were beginning to appear all over her body. With her hips paralysed by arthritis, her right arm half powerless and her left immovably fixed to the intravenous dripper, she could not make the first beginnings of a movement.

'Pull me up,' she said.

I dared not, all by myself. I was not worried by her nakedness any more: it was no longer my mother, but a poor tormented body. Yet I was frightened by the horrible mystery that I sensed, without in any way visualizing anything, under the dressings, and I was afraid of hurting her. That morning she had had to have another enema and Mademoiselle Leblon had needed my help. I took hold of that skeleton clothed in damp blue skin, holding under the armpits. When Maman was laid over on her side, her face screwed up, her eyes turned back and she cried, 'I am going to fall.' She was remembering the time she had fallen down. Standing by the side of her bed I held her and comforted her.

We sat her up again, carefully propped with pillows. After a moment she exclaimed, 'I have broken wind!' A little later she cried, 'Quick! The bed-pan.'

Mademoiselle Leblon and a red-haired nurse tried to put her on to a bed-pan; she cried out;

seeing her raw flesh and the harsh gleam of the metal, I had the impression that they were setting her down on knife-edges. The two women urged her, pulled her about, and the red-haired nurse was rough with her; Maman cried out, her body tense with pain. 'Ah! Leave her alone!' I said.

I went out with the nurses. 'It doesn't matter. Let her do it in her bed.'

'But it is so humiliating,' protested Mademoiselle Leblon. 'Patients cannot bear it.'

'And she will be soaked,' said the red-head. 'It is very bad for her bed-sores.'

'You can change the clothes at once,' I said.

I went back to Maman. 'That red-haired one is an evil woman,' she moaned in her little girl's voice. And much distressed she added, 'Still, I didn't think I was a cry-baby.'

'You aren't one.' And I said to her, 'You don't have to bother about a bed-pan. They will change the sheets—there's no sort of difficulty about it.'

'Yes,' she replied. And with a frown and a look of determination on her face she said, as though she were uttering a challenge, 'The dead certainly do it in their beds.'

This took me completely aback. 'It is so humiliating.' And Maman, who had lived a life bristling with proud sensitivities, felt no shame. In this prim and spiritualistic woman it was also a form of courage to take on our animality with so much decision.

She was changed, cleaned and rubbed with alcohol. Now it was time for her to have a quite painful injection that was meant, I think, to counteract the urea, which she was not getting rid of properly. She seemed so exhausted that Mademoiselle Leblon hesitated. 'Do it,' said Maman, 'since it's good for me.'

Once more we turned her over on to her side; I held her and I watched her face, which showed a mixture of confused distress, courage, hope and anguish. 'Since it is good for me.' In order to get well. In order to die. I should have liked to beg someone to forgive me.

The next day I learnt that the afternoon had passed off well. A young male nurse had taken Mademoiselle Leblon's place and Poupette said to Maman, 'How lucky you are to have such a young, kind nurse.'

'Yes,' said Maman, 'he's a good-looking fellow.'

'And you are a judge of men!'

'Oh, not much of a judge,' said Maman, with nostalgia in her voice.

'You have regrets?'

Maman laughed and said, 'I always say to my grand-nieces, "My dears, make the most of your life." '

'Now I understand why they love you so much. But you would never have said that to your daughters?'

'To my daughters?' said Maman, with sudden severity. 'Certainly not!'

Dr P had brought her an eighty-year-old woman on whom he was to operate the next day and who was frightened: Maman lectured her, setting forth her own case as an example.

'They are using me as an advertisement,' she

told me in an amused voice on Monday. She asked me, 'Has my right side come back? I really do have a right side?'

'Of course you have. Look at yourself,' said my sister.

Maman fixed an unbelieving, severe and haughty gaze upon the mirror. 'Is that me?'

'Why, yes. You can see that all your face is there.'

'It is quite grey.'

'That's the light. You are really pink.'

She did in fact look very well. Nevertheless, when she smiled at Mademoiselle Leblon she said to her, 'Ah! This time I smiled at you with the whole of my mouth. Before, I only had half a smile.'

In the afternoon she was not smiling any more. Several times she repeated, in a surprised and blaming voice, 'When I saw myself in the mirror I thought I was so ugly!' The night before, something had gone wrong with the intravenous drip: the tube had had to be taken out and then thrust back into the vein. The night-nurse had fumbled, the liquid had flowed under the skin and it had hurt Maman very much. Her blue and hugely swollen arm was swathed in bandages. The apparatus was now attached to her right arm: her tired veins could just put up with the serum, but the plasma forced groans from her. In the evening an intense anxiety came over her: she was afraid of the night, of some fresh accident, of pain. With her face all tense she begged, 'Watch over the drip very carefully!' And that evening too, as I looked at her arm, into which there was flowing a life that was no longer anything but sickness and torment, I asked myself *why*?

At the nursing-home I did not have time to go into it. I had to help Maman to spit; I had to give her something to drink, arrange her pillows or her plait, move her leg, water her flowers, open the window, close it, read her the paper, answer her questions, wind up the watch that lay on her chest, hanging from a black ribbon. She took a pleasure in her dependence and she called for our attention all the time. But when I reached home, all the sadness and horror of these last days dropped upon me with all its weight. And I too had a cancer eating into me—remorse. 'Don't let them operate on her.' And I had not prevented anything. Often, hearing of sick people undergoing a long martyrdom, I had felt indignant at the apathy of their relatives. 'For my part, I should kill him.' At the first trial I had given in: beaten by the ethics of society, I had abjured my own. 'No,' Sartre said to me. 'You were beaten by technique: and that was fatal.' Indeed it was. One is caught up in the wheels and dragged along, powerless in the face of specialists' diagnoses, their forecasts, their decisions. The patient becomes their property: get him away from them if you can! There were only two things to choose between on that Wednesday—operating or euthanasia. Maman, vigorously resuscitated, and having a strong heart, would have stood out against the intestinal stoppage for a long while and she would have lived through hell, for the doctors would have refused euthanasia. I ought to have been there at six in the morning. But even so, would I have dared say to N, 'Let her go'? That was what I was suggesting when I begged, 'Do not torment her', and he had snubbed me with all the arrogance of a man who is certain of his duty. They would have said to me, 'You may be depriving her of several years of life.' And I was forced to yield. These arguments did not bring me peace. The future horrified me. When I was fifteen my uncle Maurice died of cancer of the stomach. I was told that for days on end he shrieked 'Finish me off. Give me my revolver. Have pity on me.' Would Dr P keep his promise: 'She shall not suffer'? A race had begun between death and torture. I asked myself how one manages to go on living when someone you love has called out to you 'Have pity on me' in vain.

And even if death were to win, all this odious deception! Maman thought that we were with her, next to her; but we were already placing ourselves on the far side of her history. An evil all-knowing spirit, I could see behind the scenes, while she was struggling, far, far away, in human loneliness. Her desperate eagerness to get well, her patience, her courage—it was all deceived. She would not be paid for any of her sufferings at all. I saw her face again: 'Since it is good for me.' Despairingly, I suffered a transgression that was mine without my being responsible for it and one that I could never expiate.

Maman had passed a quiet night: the nurse,

seeing her anxiety, had held her hand all the time. They had found a way of putting her on the bed-pan without hurting her. She was beginning to eat again and presently the infusions would be stopped. 'This evening!' she begged.

'This evening or tomorrow,' said N.

In these circumstances there would still be a night-nurse, but my sister would sleep at her friends' house. I asked Dr P's advice. Sartre was taking the plane for Prague the next day: should I go with him? 'Anything at all can happen, and at any time. But this state of affairs can also last for months. You would never get away. Prague is only an hour and a half from Paris, and telephoning is easy.'

I spoke to Maman about the plan. 'Of course you must go! I don't need you,' she said. My going finally convinced her that she was out of danger. 'I was very far gone! Peritonitis at seventy-eight! What luck that I was here! What luck they hadn't operated on my leg.' Her left arm, free of its bandages, had gone down a little. Carefully she raised her hand to her face and touched her nose, her mouth. 'I had the feeling that my eyes were in the middle of my cheeks and that my nose was right down at the bottom of my face, all bent. It's odd . . .'

Maman had not been in the habit of taking notice of herself. Now her body forced itself upon her attention. Ballasted with this weight, she no longer floated in the clouds and she no longer said anything that shocked me. When she spoke of the Boucicaut, it was to say how sorry she was for the patients who were con-

demned to a public ward. She was on the side
of the nurses against the management, which
was exploiting them. In spite of the gravity of
her condition she never varied from the careful
consideration that she had always shown. She
was afraid of giving Mademoiselle Leblon too
much work. She said thank you; she apologized
—'All this blood they are using on an old woman,
when there are young people who might need
it!' She blamed herself for taking up my time.
'You have things to do, and you spend hours
and hours here: it vexes me!' There was some
pride, but there was also remorse in her voice
when she said, 'My poor dears! I have upset
you! You must have been terrified.' Her anxiety
extended to us, too. On Thursday morning,
when the maid brought my sister's breakfast,
Maman was scarcely out of her coma, but she
whispered, 'Conf . . . conf . . .'

'Confessor?'

'No. *Confiture.*' She was remembering that
my sister liked jam for breakfast.

She was deeply concerned about the sales of
my last book. As Mademoiselle Leblon was
being evicted by her landlord, Maman agreed
with my sister's suggestion that she should stay
at the studio: usually she could not bear the
idea of anyone going into her place when she
was not there. Her illness had quite broken the
shell of her prejudices and her pretensions:
perhaps because she no longer needed these
defences. No question of renunciation or sacrifice any more: her first duty was to get better
and so to look after herself; giving herself up

to her own wishes and her own pleasures with
no holding back, she was at last freed from resentment. Her restored beauty and her recovered smile expressed her inner harmony and,
on this death-bed, a kind of happiness.

We noticed, and we were rather surprised
at it, that she had not asked that her confessor,
who had been put off on Tuesday, should come
again. Well before her operation she had said
to Marthe, 'Pray for me, my dear, because when
you are ill, you know, you can't pray any more.'
No doubt she was too much taken up with getting well to undergo the fatigues of religious
practices. One day Dr N said to her, 'Recovering as quickly as this must mean that you are
on good terms with God!'

'Oh, we get along very well. But I don't want
to go and see Him right away.'

The earthly meaning of eternal life was
death, and she refused to die. Of course, her
devout friends thought that we were going
against her wishes, and they tried to force matters. In spite of the notice No Visitors, one
morning my sister saw a priest's cassock in the
opening door: she briskly thrust him back. 'I am
Father Avril. I have come as a friend.'

'I don't mind. Your clothes would frighten
Maman.'

On Monday, a fresh intrusion. 'Maman cannot see anyone,' said my sister, drawing Madame
de Saint-Ange into the lobby.

'Very well. But I must discuss a very serious
question with you: I know your mother's be-
liefs . . .'

'I know them too,' replied my sister curtly. 'Maman has all her faculties. The day she asks to see a priest she shall do so.'

When I left for Prague on Wednesday morning she had still not asked for one.

AT NOON I telephoned. 'Haven't you gone, then?'
said Poupette, so clearly did she hear me.
Maman was very well; on Thursday, too; on
Friday she talked to me, pleased that I should
be calling her from so far away. She was reading a little, and doing crosswords. On Saturday
I was not able to telephone. At half past eleven
on Sunday evening I asked for the Diatos' number: while I was waiting in my bedroom for the
call to be put through, I was brought a tele-
gram. 'Maman very ill. Can you come back?'
Francine told me that Poupette was spending
the night at the clinic. A little while after I got
through to her. 'A dreadful day,' she told me.
'I held Maman's hand all the time and she kept
begging me not to let her go. She said, "I shall
not see Simone again." Now they have given
her equanil and she is sleeping.'

I asked the porter to reserve me a place in
the aeroplane that was leaving the next morning
at half past ten. Engagements had been fixed;
Sartre advised me to wait a day or two. Impossible. I did not particularly want to see Maman
again before her death; but I could not bear
the idea that she should not see me again. Why

attribute such importance to a moment since there would be no memory? There would not be any atonement either. For myself I understood, to the innermost fibre of my being, that the absolute could be enclosed within the last moments of a dying person.

At half past one on Monday I walked into room 114. Maman had been told of my coming back, and she thought it was in line with my plans. She took off her dark glasses and smiled at me. Under the effect of the tranquillizers she was in a state of euphoria. Her face had changed; its colour was yellow and a puffy fold ran down from under her right eye along her nose. Yet there were flowers again on all the tables. Mademoiselle Leblon had gone; Maman no longer needed a private nurse since the intravenous drip had been stopped. The evening I left, Mademoiselle Leblon had begun a transfusion that was meant to go on for two hours: Maman's overburdened veins could bear blood even less than they could bear plasma. She cried out for five minutes on end. 'Stop!' Poupette had said. The nurse resisted. 'What will Dr N say?' 'I take full responsibility.' N was indeed very angry. 'The cicatrization will be slower.' Yet he knew very well that the wound would not close; it was forming a fistula through which the intestine was emptying itself—it was that which was preventing a fresh blockage, for the intestinal motion, the 'traffic', had stopped. How long would Maman hold out? According to the analyses the tumour was an extremely virulent sarcoma which had begun to disseminate throughout the organism: in view of her age, however, the development might be quite slow.

She told me about her last two days. On Saturday she had begun a novel by Simenon and had beaten Poupette at crosswords—there was a pile of the squares that she cut out of the papers on her table. On Sunday she had had mashed potatoes for lunch which had not gone down properly (in fact it was the beginning of the metastases that played havoc with her) and she had a long waking nightmare. 'I was in a blue sheet, over a hole; your sister was holding the sheet and I begged her, "Don't let me fall into the hole . . ." "I am holding you; you will not fall," said Poupette.'

Poupette had spent the night sitting up in an armchair and Maman, who was usually anxious about Poupette's sleep, said, 'Stay awake; don't let me go. If I go to sleep, wake me up; don't let me go while I am sleeping.' At one moment, my sister told me, Maman closed her eyes, exhausted. Her hands clawed the sheets and she articulated, 'Live! Live!'

To spare her this anguish, the doctors had prescribed pills, and injections of equanil; Maman avidly insisted upon having them. She was in an excellent mood all day long. Again she picked upon the strangeness of her impressions. 'There was a tiresome round opposite me. Your sister could not see it. I said to her, "Cover that round." She could not see any round.' It was a little metal plate set in the window-frame and it had been covered by pulling down the blind a little—they had at last repaired it. She had seen Chantal and Catherine, and in a satisfied tone she told us, 'Dr P said to me that I had been very clever. I have managed things very cleverly—while I am getting over my operation my femur is joining up again.' In the evening I suggested taking my sister's place, for she had scarcely closed her eyes the night before; but Maman was used to her; and she thought her much more competent than me, since she had looked after Lionel.

The day of Tuesday passed off well. In the night Maman had horrible dreams. 'They put me in a box,' she said to my sister. 'I am here, but I am in the box. I am myself, and yet it is not me any longer. Men carry the box away!' She struggled. 'Don't let them carry me away!'

For a long while Poupette kept her hand on Maman's forehead. 'I promise. They shall not put you in the box.'

She asked for an extra dose of equanil. Saved from her visions at last, Maman questioned her. 'But what does it all mean, this box, and these men?'

'They are memories of your operation: male nurses carried you on a stretcher.'

Maman went to sleep. But in the morning there was all the sadness of a defenceless animal in her eyes. When the nurses made her bed, and then made her urinate with a catheter, it hurt her and she groaned: in a faint voice she asked me, 'Do you think I shall come through?'

I scolded her. Timidly she questioned Dr N. 'Are you pleased with me?'

He answered yes without the least conviction, but she clung to this lifebuoy. She always discovered excellent reasons to justify her extreme weariness. There had been dehydration; the mashed potatoes were too heavy; on that particular day she blamed the nurses for only having given her three dressings instead of four the day before. 'Dr N was furious, in the evening,' she said. 'How he blew them up!' Several times she repeated, 'He was furious!' in a satisfied tone. Her face had lost its beauty; it jerked with nervous tics; rancour and demandingness showed through in her voice once again.

'I am so very tired,' she sighed. She had agreed to see Marthe's brother, a young Jesuit, in the afternoon.

'Would you like me to put him off?'

'No. Your sister will like to see him. They will talk theology. I shall close my eyes: I won't have to talk.'

She ate no lunch. She went to sleep, with her head drooping forward: when Poupette opened the door she thought it was all over. Charles Cordonnier only stayed five minutes. He spoke of the luncheons to which his father used to invite Maman every week. 'I certainly expect to see you in the boulevard Raspail again, one of these Thursdays.'

She gazed at him, incredulous and distressed. 'Do you think I shall go there again?'

I had never yet seen such a look of unhappiness on her face: that day she guessed that there was no hope for her. We thought the end so close that when Poupette came I did not go.

'So I am getting worse, since you are both here,' she murmured.

'We are always here.'

'Not both at the same time.'

Once again I pretended to be cross. 'I'm staying because you are low in your spirits. But if it only worries you, I'll go away.'

'No, no,' she said, in a downcast voice.

My unfair harshness wrung my heart. At the time the truth was crushing her and when she needed to escape from it by talking, we were condemning her to silence; we forced her to say nothing about her anxieties and to suppress her doubts: as it had so often happened in her life, she felt both guilty and misunderstood. But we had no choice: hope was her most urgent need. Chantal and Catherine had been so frightened by her appearance that they had telephoned to Limoges to advise their mother to come back.

Poupette was utterly tired out. 'I am going to sleep here tonight,' I decided.

Maman looked uneasy. 'Will you be able to manage? Will you know how to put your hand on my forehead if I have nightmares?'

'Of course I will.'

She thought it over; she looked at me intently. 'You frighten me, you do.'

I had always rather intimidated Maman because of the intellectual esteem that she had for me, and that she resolutely declined to have for her younger daughter. It worked the other way too: her prudishness had frozen me at a very early age. As a child I was a frank little girl; and then I saw the way grown-ups lived, each shut up inside little private walls; sometimes Maman made a hole in the walls, a hole that was quickly plugged up again. 'She told me in confidence,' whispered Maman with a consequential air. Or a crack was discovered from outside. 'She is very close, and she told me nothing; but it seems that . . .' The confessions and the gossip had something furtive about them that I found revolting, and I wanted my ramparts to be impregnable. I was particularly diligent in giving away nothing to Maman, out of fear of her distress and horror of having her peer into me. Soon she no longer ventured to ask questions. Our brief confrontation on my loss of faith cost us both a great deal. The sight of her tears grieved me; but I soon realized that she was weeping over her failure, without caring about what was happening inside me. And she antagonized me by preferring the force of authority to friendliness. We might still have come to an understanding if, instead of asking everybody to pray for my soul, she had given me a little confidence and sympathy. I know now what prevented her from doing so: she had too much to pay back, too many wounds to salve, to put herself in another's place. In actual doing she made every sacrifice, but her feelings did not take her out of herself. Besides, how could she have tried to understand me since she avoided looking into her own heart? As for discovering an attitude that would not have set us apart, nothing in her life had ever prepared her for such a thing: the unexpected sent her into a panic, because she had been taught never to think, act or feel except in a ready-made framework.

The silence between us became quite impenetrable. Until *She Came to Stay* came out she knew almost nothing at all about my life.

She tried to persuade herself that at least as far as morals were concerned I was 'a good girl'. Public rumour destroyed her illusions; but at that particular time our relationship had changed. She was financially dependent upon me; she took no practical decision without consulting me; I was the family's breadwinner—her son, as it were. Then again, I was a well-known writer. These circumstances to some degree excused the irregularity of my life, which in any case she minimized—a free union was, after all, less impious than a civil marriage. She was often shocked by what was in my books; but she was flattered by their success. But this, by giving me authority in her eyes, made her conflict worse. It was useless for me to avoid all argument—or maybe for the very reason that I did avoid it, she thought that I was sitting in judgment on her. Poupette, 'the baby', was less respected than I was; she had been less marked by Maman, and so she had not inherited her stiffness; and she had a freer relationship with her. Poupette undertook to give her all the comforting assurances that could be thought of when my *Memoirs of a Dutiful Daughter* came out. For my part, I confined myself to taking her a bunch of flowers and making the simplest apology: I may add that this moved and astonished her. One day she said to me, 'Parents do not understand their children; but it works both ways . . .' We talked about these misunderstandings, but in a general way. And we never returned to the question. I would knock. I would hear a little moaning noise, the scuffling of her slippers on the floor, another sigh; and

I would promise myself that this time I should find things to talk about, a common ground of understanding. By the end of five minutes the game was lost: we had so few shared interests! I leafed through her books: we did not read the same ones. I made her talk; I listened to her; I commented. But since she was my mother, her unpleasant phrases irked me more than if they had come from any other mouth. And I was as rigid as I had been at twenty when she tried (with her usual clumsiness) to move on to an intimate plane. 'I know you don't think me intelligent; but still, you get your vitality from me. The idea makes me happy.' I should have been delighted to agree that my vitality came from her; but the beginning of her remark utterly chilled me. So we each paralysed the other. It was all that that she meant, when she looked firmly at me and said, 'You frighten me, you do.'

I put on my sister's nightdress; I lay down on the couch beside Maman's bed: for my part, too, I was apprehensive. As the evening came on, the room grew dismal; it was lit only by the bedside lamp, for Maman had had the blind pulled down. I felt that the gloom made its funereal mystery even deeper. In fact, I slept better that night, and the three that followed it, than at home, for I was shielded from the anxiety of the telephone and from the wild running of my imagination: I was there; I thought of nothing.

Maman had no nightmares. The first night she often woke and asked for a drink. The second, her coccyx hurt her a great deal: Mademoiselle Cournot laid her on her right side, but then her arm tortured her. They set her on a round rubber cushion, which eased the place that hurt; but there was the danger that it might harm the skin of her buttocks, such frail, blue skin. On Friday and Saturday she slept quite well. From the day of Thursday onwards she had regained her confidence, thanks to the equanil. She no longer asked, 'Do you think I will come through?' but 'Do you think I shall be able to go back to a normal life?'

'Ah, today I can see you!' she said to me in a happy voice. 'Yesterday I couldn't see you at all.'

The next day Jeanne, who had come up from Limoges, found her looking less ravaged than she had feared. They chatted for nearly an hour. When she came back on Saturday morning with Chantal, Maman said to them gaily, 'Well, my funeral isn't for tomorrow! I shall live to be a hundred: they will have to put me down.'

Dr P was puzzled. 'There is no possible forecast with her; she has such immense vitality.'

I told Maman of his last remark. 'Yes, I have plenty of vitality,' she observed with pleasure. She was rather surprised: her bowels were not working any more, and yet the doctors did not seem to worry.

'The main thing is that they have worked: that proves they are not paralysed. The doctors are very pleased.'

'If they are pleased, that's all that matters.'

On Saturday evening we talked before going to sleep. 'It's very odd,' she said in a thoughtful tone, 'but when I think of Mademoiselle Leblon,

I see her in my flat: she's a kind of swollen dummy with no arms, like those you see in dry-cleaners'. Dr P is a strip of black paper on my stomach. So when I see him in the flesh, it seems very odd to me.'

I said to her, 'You have got used to me, you see: I don't frighten you any more.'

'Of course not.'

'But you said I frightened you.'

'I said that? One says the strangest things.'

I, too, grew used to this way of life. I arrived at eight in the evening; Poupette told me how the day had passed; Dr N came by. Mademoiselle Cournot appeared, and I read in the lobby while she changed the dressing. Four times a day, a table loaded with bandages, gauze, linen, cotton-wool, sticking-plaster, tins, basins and scissors was wheeled into the room; I studiously looked away when it was wheeled out again. Mademoiselle Cournot, helped by a nurse she knew, washed Maman and made her ready for the night. I went to bed. She gave Maman various injections, and then she went off to drink a cup of coffee, while I read by the light of the bedside lamp. She came back and sat down near the door, which she left ajar so that a little light should come through from the entrance corridor: she read and knitted. There was the slight sound of the electric apparatus that caused the mattress to vibrate. I went to sleep. At seven, time to get up. During the dressing of the wound I turned my face to the wall, thanking my good fortune I had a cold that was blocking my nose: Poupette had suffered from the smell, but for my part I was aware of almost nothing, except for the scent of the eau de Cologne that I often put on Maman's forehead and cheeks, and that seemed to me sweetish and sickening: I shall never be able to use that brand again.

Mademoiselle Cournot left; I dressed; I ate my breakfast. I prepared a whitish medicine for Maman; it was very unpleasant, she said, but it helped her digestion. Then, spoon by spoon, I gave her tea in which I had crumbled a biscuit. The maid swept and dusted. I watered the flowers and arranged them. The telephone-bell rang often; I hurried into the lobby. I closed the doors behind me, but I was not sure whether Maman could hear and I spoke cautiously. She laughed when I told her, 'Madame Raymond asked me how your femur was getting on.'

'They don't understand anything about it.'

Often, too, a nurse would call me: friends of Maman's, and relations, came to ask after her. Generally, she was not strong enough to see them, but she was very pleased at the attention. I went out during the dressing. Then I helped her have lunch: she could not chew, and she ate mashed vegetables, gruel, very finely chopped mince, stewed fruit, custard: she forced herself to empty her plate. 'I must feed myself up.' Between meals, she drank a mixture of fresh fruit juices in little sips. 'There are vitamins in it. They're good for me.' Poupette came at about two o'clock: 'I like this routine very much,' said Maman. One day she said to us regretfully, 'How stupid! Now that for once I have you both with me, I am ill!'

I was calmer than before Prague. The transition from my mother to a living corpse had been definitively accomplished. The world had shrunk to the size of her room: when I crossed Paris in a taxi I saw nothing more than a stage with extras walking about on it. My real life took place at her side, and it had only one aim— protecting her. In the night the slightest sound seemed huge to me—the rustling of Mademoiselle Cournot's paper, the purring of the electric motor. I walked in stockinged feet in the daytime. The coming and going on the staircase, and overhead, shattered my ears. The din of the wheeled tables that went by on the landing between eleven o'clock and noon, loaded with clattering metal trays, cans and bowls, seemed to me scandalous. I was furious when a thoughtless maid asked Maman, when she was dozing, to say which she would like to eat the next day, sautéd rabbit or roast chicken. And again, when at lunch-time, she was brought an unappetizing mince instead of the promised brains. I shared Maman's likings; we were in favour of Mademoiselle Cournot, Mademoiselle Laurent and the girls called Martin and Parent; I, too, thought Madame Gontrand over-talkative. 'She told me that she spent her afternoon off buying shoes for her daughter: what's that to me?'

We no longer liked this nursing-home. The smiling, painstaking nurses were overwhelmed with work, badly paid, harshly treated. Mademoiselle Cournot brought her own coffee; she was not provided with anything more than the hot water. The night-nurses had no shower, nor even a washroom where they could wash and make themselves up again after a sleepless night. Mademoiselle Cournot, quite upset, told us one morning about her differences with the sister, who blamed her for wearing brown shoes.

'They have no heels,' said Mademoiselle Cournot.

'They have to be white.'

Mademoiselle Cournot looked miserable. 'Don't put on that weary expression before you have even begun your day's work,' cried the sister.

Maman repeated that phrase over and over again for two days: she had always delighted in taking sides very strongly. One evening Mademoiselle Cournot's friend came into the room, crying: her patient had decided not to speak to her any more. Their profession brought these girls into very close touch with tragedies; but that did not harden them at all against the little dramas of their personal life.

'You feel yourself growing half-witted,' said Poupette.

For my part I put up with the silliness of the conversations, the ritual facetiousness—'That was a good trick you played on Professor B!' 'With those dark glasses you look just like Greta Garbo!'—with indifference. But the words went bad in my mouth. I had the feeling of play-acting wherever I went. When I spoke to an old friend about her forthcoming removal, the liveliness in my voice seemed to me phoney: when with perfect truth I observed 'That was very good' to the manager of a restaurant, I had the impression of telling a white lie. At other times it was the outside world that seemed to be acting a part. I saw a hotel as a nursing-home; I took the chambermaids for nurses; and the restaurant waitresses too—they were making me follow a course of treatment that consisted of eating. I looked at people with a fresh eye, obsessed by the complicated system of tubes that was concealed under their clothing. Sometimes I myself turned into a lift-and-force pump or into a sequence of pockets and guts.

Poupette was living on her nerves. My blood-pressure mounted; a pulse throbbed in my head. What tried us more than anything were Maman's death-agonies, her resurrections, and our own inconsistency. In this race between pain and death we most earnestly hoped that death would come first. Yet when Maman was asleep with her face lifeless, we would anxiously gaze at the white bed-jacket to catch the faint movement of the black ribbon that held her watch: dread of the last spasm gripped us by the throat.

She was well when I left her in the early afternoon of Sunday. On Monday morning her wasted face terrified me; it was terribly obvious, the work of those mysterious colonies between her skin and her bones that were devouring her cells. At ten in the evening Poupette had secretly passed the nurse a piece of paper—'Should I call my sister?' The nurse shook her head: Maman's heart was holding out. But new forms of wretchedness were to come. Madame Gontrand showed me Maman's right side: water dripped from the pores of her skin; the sheet was soaked. She hardly urinated any more and her flesh was puffing up in an oedema. She looked at her hands, and in a puzzled way she moved her swollen fingers. 'It is because you have to keep so still,' I told her.

Tranquillized by equanil and morphia, she was aware of her sickness, but she accepted it patiently. 'One day when I thought I was better already your sister said something that has been very useful to me: she said that I should be unwell again. So I know that it's normal.' She saw Madame de Saint-Ange for a moment and said to her, 'Oh, now I am coming along very well!' A smile uncovered her gums: already it was the macabre grin of a skeleton; at the same time her eyes shone with a somewhat feverish innocence. She was suddenly unwell after having eaten; I rang and rang for the nurse; what I had wanted was happening; she was dying and it filled me with panic. A tablet brought her round.

In the evening I imagined her dead, and it wrung my heart. 'Things are going rather better locally,' Poupette told me in the morning, and I regretted it bitterly. Maman was so well that she read a few pages of Simenon. In the night she suffered a great deal. 'I hurt all over!' They gave her an injection of morphia. When she opened her eyes during the day they had an unseeing, glassy look and I thought, 'This time it is the end.' She went to sleep again. I asked N, 'Is this the end?'

'Oh, no!' he said in a half-pitying, half triumphant tone, 'she has been revived too well for that!'

So it was to be pain that would win? *Finish me off. Give me my revolver. Have pity on me.* She said, 'I hurt all over.' She moved her swollen

fingers anxiously. Her confidence waned: 'These
doctors are beginning to irritate me. They are
always telling me that I am getting better. And
I feel myself getting worse.'

I had grown very fond of this dying woman.
As we talked in the half-darkness I assuaged
an old unhappiness; I was renewing the dia-
logue that had been broken off during my adolescence and that our differences and our like-
nesses had never allowed us to take up again.
And the early tenderness that I had thought
dead for ever came to life again, since it had
become possible for it to slip into simple words
and actions.

I looked at her. She was there, present, conscious, and completely unaware of what she
was living through. Not to know what is happening underneath one's skin is normal enough.
But for her the outside of her body was unknown—her wounded abdomen, her fistula, the
filth that issued from it, the blueness of her
skin, the liquid that oozed out of her pores: she
could not explore it with her almost paralysed
hands, and when they treated her and dressed
her wound her head was thrown back. She had
not asked for a mirror again: her dying face
did not exist for her. She rested and dreamed,
infinitely far removed from her rotting flesh,
her ears filled with the sound of our lies; her
whole person was concentrated upon one passionate hope—getting well. I should have liked
to spare her pointless unpleasantnesses: 'You
don't have to take this medicine any more.' 'It
would be better to take it.' And she gulped
down the chalky liquid. She found it difficult

to eat: 'Don't force yourself: that's enough; don't eat any more.' 'Do you think so?' She looked at the dish, hesitated, 'Give me a little more.' In the end I spirited her plate away: 'You finished it all up,' I said. She compelled herself to swallow yoghourt in the afternoon. She often asked for fruit-juice. She moved her arms a little, and slowly, carefully raised her hands, cupping them together, and gropingly she seized the glass, which I still held. She drew up the beneficent vitamins through the little tube: a ghoul's mouth avidly sucking life.

Her eyes had grown huge in her wasted face; she opened them wide, fixed them; at the cost of an immense effort she wrenched herself from her dim private world to rise to the surface of those pools of dark light; she concentrated her whole being there; she gazed at me with a dramatic immobility—it was as though she had just discovered sight. 'I can see you!' Every time she had to win it from the darkness again. By her eyes she clung to the world, as by her nails she clung to the sheet, so that she might not be engulfed. 'Live! Live!'

How desolate I was, that Wednesday evening, in the cab that was taking me away! I knew this journey through the fashionable quarters by heart: Lancôme, Houbigant, Hermès, Lanvin. Often a red light stopped me in front of Cardin's: I saw ridiculously elegant hats, waistcoats, scarves, slippers, shoes. Farther on there were beautiful downy dressing-gowns, softly coloured: I thought, 'I will buy her one to take the place of the red peignoir.' Scents, furs, lingerie, jewels: the sumptuous arrogance of a world in which death had no place: but it was there, lurking behind this façade, in the grey secrecy of nursing-homes, hospitals, sick-rooms. And for me that was now the only truth.

On Thursday Maman's face shocked me, as it did every day: it was a little hollower and more tormented than the day before. But she could see. She examined me: 'I am looking at you. Your hair is quite brown.'

'Of course it is. You have always known that.'

'Because both you and your sister had a broad white streak. It was so that I could hold on, not to fall.' She moved her fingers. 'They are going down, aren't they?' She went to sleep. As she opened her eyes she said to me, 'When I see a big white wristband I know I am going to wake up. When I go to sleep, I go to sleep in petticoats.' What memories, what phantasms were invading her? Her life had always been turned towards the outward world and I found it very moving to see her suddenly lost within herself. She no longer liked to be distracted. That day a friend, Mademoiselle Vauthier, told her an anecdote about a charwoman, with too much liveliness altogether. I quickly got rid of her, for Maman was closing her eyes. When I came back she said, 'You ought not to tell sick people stories of that kind; it does not interest them.'

I spent that night beside her. She was as much afraid of the nightmares as she was of pain. When Dr N came she begged, 'Let them inject me as often as necessary,' and she imitated the action of a nurse thrusting in the needle.

'Ha, ha, you are going to become a real drug-addict!' said N in a bantering tone. 'I can supply you with morphia at very interesting rates.' His expression hardened and he coldly said in my direction, 'There are two points upon which a self-respecting doctor does not compromise—drugs and abortion.'

Friday passed uneventfully. On Saturday Maman slept all the time. 'That's splendid,' said Poupette to her. 'You have rested.'

'Today I have not lived,' sighed Maman.

A hard task, dying, when one loves life so much. 'She may hold out for two or three months,' the doctors told us that evening. So we had to organize our lives and get Maman used to spending a few hours without us. As her husband had come to Paris the day before, my sister decided to leave Maman alone that night with Mademoiselle Cournot. She would come in the morning; Marthe would come at about half past two; and I would come at five.

At five I opened the door. The blind was down and it was almost entirely dark. Marthe was holding Maman's hand, and Maman was lying crumpled up, on her right side, with a pitiful, exhausted look: the bed-sores on her left buttock were completely raw and lying like this she suffered less, but the discomfort of her position was tiring her out. She had waited in extreme anxiety until eleven o'clock for Poupette and Lionel to come, because the nurses had forgotten to pin the bell-cord to her sheet: the push button was out of her reach and she had no way of calling anyone. Her friend, Madame Tardieu, had come to see her, but all the same

Maman said to my sister, 'You leave me in the power of the brutes!' (She hated the Sunday nurses.) Then she recovered enough spirit to say to Lionel, 'So you hoped to be rid of mother-in-law? Well, it's not to be; not yet.' She was alone for an hour after lunch and the tormenting anxiety seized upon her again. In a feverish voice she said to me, 'I must not be left alone; I am still too weak. I must not be left in the power of the brutes!'

'We won't leave you any more.'

Marthe went away; Maman dozed off and woke with a start—her right buttock was hurting. Madame Gontrand changed her. Maman still complained: I wanted to ring again. 'It would still be Madame Gontrand. She's no good.' There was nothing imaginary about Maman's pains; they had exact organic causes. Yet below a certain threshold they could be soothed by the attentions of Mademoiselle Parent or Mademoiselle Martin; exactly the same things done by Madame Gontrand did not ease her. However, she went to sleep again. At half past six she took some soup and custard, and it gave her pleasure. Then suddenly she cried out, a burning pain in her left buttock. It was not at all surprising. Her flayed body was bathing in the uric acid that oozed from her skin; the nurses burnt their fingers when they changed her draw-sheet. I rang and rang, panic-stricken: how the interminable seconds dragged out! I held Maman's hand, I stroked her forehead, I talked. 'They will give you an injection. It won't hurt any more. Just one minute more. Only one minute.' All tense, on the edge of shrieking, she moaned, 'It burns, it's awful; I can't stand it. I can't bear it any longer.' And half sobbing, 'I'm so utterly miserable,' in that child's voice that pierced me to the heart. How completely alone she was! I touched her, I talked to her; but it was impossible to enter into her suffering. Her heart took to beating madly, her eyes turned back, I thought 'She is dying', and she murmured, 'I am going to faint.' At last Madame Gontrand gave her an injection of morphia. It did not work. I rang again. I was terrified by the idea that the pain might have started in the morning, when Maman had no one with her and no means of calling anyone: there was no longer any question of leaving her alone for a moment. This time the nurses gave Maman equanil, changed her draw-sheet and put an ointment on her open places that left a metallic sheen on their hands. The burning went off; it had lasted only a quarter of an hour—an eternity. *He shrieked for hours.* 'It's stupid,' said Maman. 'It's so stupid.' Yes: so stupid as to make one weep. I could no longer understand the doctors, nor my sister nor myself. Nothing on earth could possibly justify these moments of pointless torment.

On Monday morning I talked to Poupette on the telephone: the end was near. The oedema was not being reabsorbed: the abdomen was not closing. The doctors had told the nurses that the only thing left to do was to daze Maman with sedatives.

At two o'clock I found my sister outside door 114, almost out of her mind. She had said to Mademoiselle Martin, 'Don't let Maman suffer

as she did yesterday.' 'But Madame, if we give
her such a lot of injections just for the bed-
sores, the morphia won't work when the time
of the great pain comes.' Questioned closely,
she explained that generally speaking, in cases
like Maman's, the patient died in hideous torment. *Have pity on me. Finish me off.* Had Dr
P lied, then? Get a revolver somehow: kill Maman: strangle her. Empty romantic fantasies.
But it was just as impossible for me to see
myself listening to Maman scream for hours.
'We'll go and talk to P.' He came and we seized
upon him. 'You promised she wouldn't suffer.'
'She will not suffer.' He pointed out that if they
had wanted to prolong her life at any cost and
give her an extra week of martyrdom, another
operation would have been necessary, together
with transfusions and resuscitating injections.
Yes. That morning even N had said to Poupette,
'We did everything that had to be done while
there was still a chance. Now it would be mere
sadism to try to delay her death.' But this
abstention was not enough for us. We asked P,
'Will morphia stop the great pains?' 'She will
be given the doses that are called for.'

He had spoken firmly and he gave us confidence. We grew calmer. He went into Maman's
room to see her dressing again. 'She's asleep,'
we told him. 'She won't even know I'm there.'
No doubt she was still asleep when he left. But
remembering her anguish of the day before I
said to Poupette, 'She mustn't wake up and find
herself alone.' My sister opened the door: she
turned back towards me, terribly pale, and collapsed on the bench, sobbing, 'I've seen her

stomach!' I went to get some equanil for her. When Dr P came back she said to him, 'I saw her stomach! It's awful!' 'Oh no,' he said, rather confused, 'it's quite normal.'

'She is rotting alive.' Poupette told me, and I asked her no questions. We talked. Then I sat by Maman's bed: I should have thought her dead but for the faint movement of the black ribbon against the whiteness of her bedjacket. At about six she opened her eyes.

'What time is it? I don't understand. Is it night already?'

'You have slept the whole afternoon.'

'I have slept forty-eight hours!'

'Oh no,' I said and I reminded her of what had happened the day before.

She looked at the darkness and the neon signs far out through the window and said, 'I don't understand,' again, in an offended voice. I told her about the visits and the telephone calls I had about her. 'It's all the same to me,' she said. She turned her surprise over and over in her mind: 'I heard the doctors: they were saying "She must be deeply sedated—dazed.'"' For once they had forgotten to be careful. I explained that there was no point in suffering as she had done yesterday; they were going to make her sleep a great deal until her bed-sores had healed over. 'Yes,' she said reproachfully, 'but these are days that I lose.'

'Today I haven't lived.' 'I am losing days.' Every day had an irreplaceable value for her. And she was going to die. She did not know it: but I did. In her name, I revolted against it.

She drank a little soup and we waited for

Poupette. 'Sleeping here tires her,' said Maman.

'I'm sure it doesn't,' I said.

She sighed. 'It's all the same to me.' And after a moment's thought, 'What worries me is that *everything* is all the same to me.' Before going to sleep again she asked me suspiciously, 'But can people be dazed, just like that?' Was it a protest? I think it was rather that she wanted me to reassure her: her torpor was brought about by drugs and it did not mean a worsening of her condition.

When Mademoiselle Cournot came in Maman opened her eyes. They wandered, but she fixed her gaze and looked steadily at the nurse with a gravity even more moving than that of a baby discovering the world.

'You, there, who are you?'

'I'm Mademoiselle Cournot.'

'Why are you here at this time of the day?'

'It is night now,' I told her again.

Her wide-open eyes questioned Mademoiselle Cournot. 'Why are you here?'

'I spend every night sitting next to you: I'm sure you remember.'

'Really! What a curious notion,' said Maman. I got ready to go. 'Are you going?'

'Would it worry you if I did?'

Once again she replied, 'It's all the same to me. Everything is the same to me.'

I did not leave at once: the day nurses said that Maman would certainly not get through the night. Her pulse leapt from forty-eight to a hundred. At about ten o'clock it steadied. Poupette lay down; I went home. I was now sure that P had not deceived us. Maman would die within a day or so without too much suffering.

She woke up clear in her mind. As soon as she felt any pain they gave her a sedative. I arrived at three: she was asleep, with Chantal by her bed.

'Poor Chantal,' she said to me a little later, 'she has so much to do, and I take up her time.'

'But she likes coming. She is so fond of you.'

Maman reflected: in a surprised, grieved voice she said, 'As for me, I no longer know whether I am fond of anyone.'

I remembered her proud 'People like me because I am cheerful.' Gradually many people had become wearisome to her. Her heart was now quite numb: tiredness had taken everything away from her. And yet not one of her most loving words had ever moved me nearly as much as this statement of indifference. Formerly the ready-made phrases and the conventional gestures had masked her real feelings. I measured their warmth by the coldness that their absence left in her.

She dropped off, and her breath was so imperceptible that I thought, 'If only it could stop, without any violence.' But the black ribbon rose and fell: the leap was not to be so easy. I woke her up at five, as she had insisted, to give her some yoghourt. 'Your sister wants me to: it's good for me.' She ate two or three spoonfuls: I thought of the food that is put on the graves of the dead in certain countries. I held her a rose to smell, one that Catherine had brought the day before—'The last of the Meyrignac roses.' She only gave it a preoccupied glance. She sank down into sleep again: a burning pain in her buttock woke her violently. Morphia injection: no result. As I had done two days before I held her hand, urged her, 'One minute more. The injection is going to work. In one minute it will be over.'

'It's a Chinese torture,' she said, in a flat, expressionless voice, too weakened even to protest.

I rang again; insisted; another injection. The Parent girl arranged the bed and moved Maman a little; she went to sleep again; her hands were deathly cold. The maid grumbled because I sent away the dinner that she brought at six o'clock: the implacable routine of clinics, where deathbeds and death itself are daily occurrences. At half past seven Maman said to me, 'Ah! Now I feel well. Really well. It's a long time since I've felt so well.' Jeanne's eldest daughter came, and she helped me give her a little soup and some coffee custard. It was difficult, because she coughed: she almost choked. Poupette and Mademoiselle Cournot advised me to leave. In all likelihood nothing would happen that night, and my being there would worry Maman. I kissed her, and with one of her hideous smiles she said to me, 'I am glad you have seen me looking so well!'

I went to bed half an hour after midnight, dosed with sleeping-pills. I woke: the telephone was ringing. 'There are only a few minutes left. Marcel is coming to fetch you in a car.' Marcel—Lionel's cousin—drove me at great speed through a deserted Paris. We gulped down some coffee at a red-lit bar near the Porte Champerret. Poupette came to meet us in the garden of the nursing-home. 'It's all over.' We went up the stairs. It was so expected and so unimaginable, that dead body lying on the bed in Maman's place. Her hand was cold; so was her forehead. It was still Maman, and it was her absence for ever. There was a bandage holding up her chin, framing her face. My sister wanted to go and fetch clothes from the rue Blomet.

'What's the point?'

'Apparently that is what's done.'

'We shan't do it.'

I could not conceive putting a dress and shoes on Maman as though she was going out to dinner; and I did not think that she would have wanted it—she had often said that she was not in the least concerned with what happened to her body.

'Just dress her in one of her long nightgowns,' I said to Mademoiselle Cournot.

'And what about her wedding-ring?' asked Poupette, taking it out of the table drawer. We put it on to her finger. Why? No doubt because that little round of gold belonged nowhere else on earth.

Poupette was utterly exhausted. After a last look at what was no longer Maman I quickly took her away. We had a drink with Marcel at the bar of the Dôme. She told us what had happened.

At nine o'clock N came out of the room and said angrily, 'Another clip has given way. After all that has been done for her: how irritating!' He went off, leaving my sister dumbfounded. In spite of her icy hands Maman complained of being too hot, and she had some difficulty in breathing. She was given an injection and she went to sleep. Poupette undressed, got into bed and went through the motions of reading a detective story. Towards midnight Maman moved about. Poupette and the nurse went to her bedside. She opened her eyes. 'What are you doing here? Why are you looking so worried? I am quite well.' 'You have been having a bad dream.' As Mademoiselle Cournot smoothed the sheets she touched Maman's feet: there was the chill of death upon them. My sister wondered whether to call me. But at that time of night my presence would have frightened Maman, whose mind was perfectly clear. Poupette went back to bed. At one o'clock Maman stirred again. In a roguish voice she whispered the words of an old refrain that Papa used to sing, *You are going away and you will leave us.* 'No, no,' said Poupette, 'I shan't leave you,' and Maman gave a little knowing smile. She found it harder and harder to breathe. After another injection she murmured in a rather thick voice, 'We must . . . keep . . . back . . . desh.'

'We must keep back the desk?'

'No,' said Maman. 'Death.' Stressing the word *death* very strongly. She added, 'I don't want to die.'

'But you are better now!'

After that she wandered a little. 'I should have liked to have the time to bring out my book . . . She must be allowed to nurse whoever she likes.'

My sister dressed herself: Maman had almost lost consciousness. Suddenly she cried, 'I can't breathe!' Her mouth opened, her eyes stared wide, huge in that wasted, ravaged face: with a spasm she entered into coma.

'Go and telephone,' said Mademoiselle Cournot.

Poupette rang me up: I did not answer. The operator went on ringing for half an hour before I woke. Meanwhile Poupette went back to Maman: already she was no longer there—her heart was beating and she breathed, sitting there with glassy eyes that saw nothing. And then it was over. 'The doctors said she would go out like a candle: it wasn't like that, it wasn't like that at all,' said my sister, sobbing.

'But, Madame,' replied the nurse, 'I assure you it was a very easy death.'

MAMAN had dreaded cancer all her life, and perhaps she was still afraid of it at the nursing-home, when they X-rayed her. After the operation she never thought of it for a single moment. There were some days when she was afraid that at her age, the shock might have been too great for her to survive it. But doubt never even touched her mind: she had been operated on for peritonitis—a grave condition, but curable.

What surprised us even more was that she never asked for a priest, not even on the day when she was so reduced and she said, 'I shall not see Simone again!' Marthe had brought her a missal, a crucifix and a rosary: she did not take them out of her drawer. One morning Jeanne said, 'It's Sunday today, Aunt Françoise: wouldn't you like to take Communion?' 'Oh, my dear, I am too tired to pray: God is kind!' Madame Tardieu asked her more pressingly, when Poupette was there, whether she would not like to see her confessor: Maman's expression hardened—'Too tired,' and she closed her eyes to put an end to the conversation. After the visit of another old friend she said to Jeanne, 'Poor dear Louise, she asks me such foolish questions: she wanted to know whether there was a chaplain in the nursing-home. Much I care whether there is or not!'

Madame de Saint-Ange harried us. 'Since she is in such a state of anxiety, she must surely want the comforts of religion.'

'But she doesn't.'

'She made me and some other friends promise to help her make a good end.'

'What she wants just now is to be helped to make a good recovery.'

We were blamed. To be sure we did not prevent Maman from receiving the last sacraments; but we did not oblige her to take them. We ought to have told her, 'You have cancer. You are going to die.' Some devout women would have done so, I am sure, if we had left them alone with her. (In their place I should have been afraid of provoking the sin of rebellion in Maman, which would have earned her centuries of purgatory.) Maman did not want these intimate conversations. What she wanted to see round her bed was young smiling faces. 'I shall have plenty of time to see other old women like me when I am in a rest-home,' she said to her grandnieces. She felt herself safe with Jeanne, Marthe and two or three religious but understanding friends who approved of our deception. She mistrusted the others and she spoke of some of them with a certain amount of ill-feeling—it was as though a surprising instinct enabled her to detect those people whose presence might disturb her peace of mind. 'As for those women at the club, I shall not go to see them again. I shall not go back there.

People may think, 'Her faith was only on the surface, a matter of words, since it did not hold out in the face of suffering and death.' I do not know what faith is. But her whole life turned upon religion; religion was its very substance: papers that we found in her desk confirm this. If she had looked upon prayer as nothing but a mechanical droning, telling her beads would not have tired her any more than doing the crossword. The fact that she did not pray convinces me that on the contrary she found it an exercise that called for concentration, thought and a certain condition of soul. She knew what she ought to have said to God—'Heal me. But Thy will be done: I acquiesce in death.' She did not acquiesce. In this moment of truth she did not choose to utter insincere words. But at the same time she did not grant herself the right to rebel. She remained silent: 'God is kind.'

'I can't understand,' said the bewildered Mademoiselle Vauthier. 'Your mother is so religious and so pious, and yet she is so afraid of death!' Did she not know that saints have died convulsed and shrieking? Besides, Maman was not afraid of either God or the Devil: only of leaving this earth. My grandmother had known perfectly well that she was dying. Contentedly she said, 'I am going to eat one last little boiled egg, and then I am going to join Gustave again.' She had never put much passion into living; at eighty-four she was gloomily vegetating; dying did not disturb or vex her. My father showed no less courage. 'Ask your mother not to get a priest to come,' he said to me, 'I don't want to act a part.' And he gave instructions on certain practical matters. Ruined, embittered, he accepted the void with the same serenity that Grandmama accepted Paradise. Maman loved life as I love it and in the face of death she had the same feeling of rebellion that I have. During her last days I received many letters with remarks on my most recent book: 'If you had not lost your faith death would not terrify you so,' wrote the devout, with rancorous commiseration. Well-intentioned readers urged, 'Disappearing is not of the least importance: your works will remain.' And inwardly I told them all that they were wrong. Religion could do no more for my mother than the hope of posthumous success could do for me. Whether you think of it as heavenly or as earthly, if you love life immortality is no consolation for death.

WHAT WOULD have happened if Maman's doctor had detected the cancer as early as the first symptoms? No doubt it would have been treated with rays and Maman would have lived two or three years longer. But she would have known or at least suspected the nature of her disease, and she would have passed the end of her life in a state of dread. What we bitterly regretted was that the doctor's mistake had deceived us; otherwise Maman's happiness would have become our chief concern. The difficulties that prevented Jeanne and Poupette from having her in the summer would not have counted. I should have seen more of her: I should have invented things to please her.

And is one to be sorry that the doctors brought her back to life and operated, or not? She, who did not want to lose a single day, 'won' thirty: they brought her joys; but they also brought her anxiety and suffering. Since she did escape from the martyrdom that I sometimes thought was hanging over her, I cannot decide for her. For my sister, losing Maman the very day she saw her again would have been a shock from which she would scarcely have recovered. And as for me? Those four weeks have left me pictures, nightmares, sadnesses that I should never have known if Maman had died that Wednesday morning. But I cannot measure the disturbance that I should have felt since my sorrow broke out in a way that I had not foreseen. We did derive an undoubted good from this respite: it saved us, or almost saved us, from remorse. When someone you love dies you pay for the sin of outliving her with a thousand piercing regrets. Her death brings to light her unique quality; she grows as vast as the world that her absence annihilates for her and whose whole existence was caused by her being there; you feel that she should have had more room in your life—all the room, if need be. You snatch yourself away from this wildness: she was only one among many. But since you never do all you might for anyone—not even within the arguable limits that you have set yourself—you have plenty of room left for self-reproach. With regard to Maman we were above all guilty, these last years, of carelessness, omission and abstention. We felt that we atoned for this by the days that we gave up to her, by the peace that our being there gave her, and by the victories gained over fear and pain. Without our obstinate watchfulness she would have suffered far more.

For indeed, comparatively speaking, her death was an easy one. 'Don't leave me in the power of the brutes.' I thought of all those who have no one to make that appeal to: what agony it must be to feel oneself a defenceless thing, utterly at the mercy of indifferent doctors and overworked nurses. No hand on the forehead when terror seizes them; no sedative as soon as pain begins to tear them; no lying prattle to fill the silence of the void. 'She aged forty years in twenty-four hours.' That phrase too had obsessed my mind. Even today—why?—there are horrible agonizing deaths. And then in the public wards, when the last hour is coming near, they put a screen round the dying man's bed: he has seen this screen round other beds that were empty the next day: he knows. I pictured Maman, blinded for hours by the black sun that no one can look at directly: the horror of her staring eyes with their dilated pupils. She had a very easy death; an upperclass death.

POUPETTE slept at my place. At ten in the morning we went back to the clinic: as in hotels, the room had to be vacated before noon. Once again we climbed the stairs, opened the two doors: the bed was empty. The walls, the window, the lamps, the furniture, everything was in its place; and on the whiteness of the sheet there was nothing. Foreseeing is not knowing: the shock was as violent as though we had not expected it at all. We took the suitcases out of the cupboard and piled in the books, linen, toilet things, papers: six weeks of an intimacy rotted by betrayal. We left the red dressing-gown behind. We crossed the garden. Somewhere at the bottom, hidden in the greenery, there was a mortuary and inside it Maman's body with the bandage round its chin. Poupette had suffered—by her own desire and also by chance—the hardest blows, and she was too overcome for me to suggest that we should go and see it again. And I was not sure that I wanted to.

We left the suitcases at the rue Blomet, with the concierge. We noticed an undertaker's. 'This will do as well as anywhere else.' Two gentle-

111

men in black asked to know our wishes. They showed us photographs of various kinds of coffin. 'This one is more aesthetic.' Poupette burst into sobbing laughter. 'More aesthetic! That box! She didn't want to be put into that box!' The burial was fixed for Friday, in two days' time. Did we want flowers? We said yes, without knowing why: not a wreath, not a cross, but a big sheaf. Very good: they would take care of everything. In the afternoon we took the suitcases up to the flat: Mademoiselle Leblon had transformed it: it was so much cleaner and more cheerful that we scarcely recognized it— so much the better. We stuffed the bag with the bedjacket and the nightdresses in it into a chest of drawers, put the books on a shelf, threw away the eau de Cologne, the sweets and the toilet things, and carried the rest to my place. That night I could not get off to sleep. I was not sorry that I had left Maman with 'I am glad you have seen me looking so well' as her last words. But I did reproach myself for having abandoned her body too soon. She, and my sister too, said, 'A corpse no longer means anything.' Yet it was her flesh, her bones, and for some time still her face. With my father I had stayed by him until the time he became a mere thing for me: I tamed the transition between presence and the void. With Maman I went away almost immediately after having kissed her, and that was why it seemed to me that it was still her that was lying, all alone, in the cold of the mortuary. The coffining would take place in the afternoon of the next day: would I go?

I was at the nursing-home at about four, to pay the bill. Post had arrived for Maman, and a bag of fruit bon-bons. I went up to say good-bye to the nurses. I found the girls, Martin and Parent, very jolly in the corridor. My throat was constricted and I could barely force out a couple of words. I went past the door of 114: they had taken down the notice 'No Visitors'. In the garden I hesitated for a moment: my courage failed me: and what was the point anyhow? I went away. I saw Cardin's again, and the beautiful dressing-gowns. I told myself that I should never sit in the lobby again, never pick up the white telephone, never make that journey any more: I should so happily have broken with those habits if Maman had been cured, but I still had a nostalgia for them, since it was in losing her that I lost them.

We wanted to give keepsakes to her closest friends. As we looked at her straw bag, filled with balls of wool and an unfinished piece of knitting, and at her blotting-pad, her scissors, her thimble, emotion rose up and drowned us. Everyone knows the power of things: life is solidified in them, more immediately present than in any one of its instants. They lay there on my table, orphaned, useless, waiting to turn into rubbish or to find another identity—my hussif, that Aunt Françoise left me. We set aside her watch for Marthe. As she undid the black ribbon Poupette began to cry. 'It's so stupid and I'm not at all a worshipper of things, but I just can't throw this ribbon away.' 'Keep it.' It is useless to try to integrate life and death and to behave rationally in the presence of something that is not rational: each must manage as well as he can in the tumult of his feelings. I can understand all last wishes and the total absence of them: the hugging of the bones or the abandonment of the body of the one you love to the common grave. If my sister had wanted to dress Maman or to keep her wedding-ring I should certainly have accepted her reactions as willingly as my own. We did not have to ask ourselves questions about the funeral. We felt we knew what Maman wanted and we kept to that.

But we came up against some macabre difficulties. We owned a perpetual concession in the Père-Lachaise cemetery, bought a hundred and thirty years before by a lady named Mignot, our great-grandfather's sister. She was buried there, as well as our grandfather, his wife, his brother, my uncle Gaston and Papa. There was no room left. In such cases the dead person is buried in a provisional grave, and when the bones of those who have been buried before are gathered into a single coffin, then there is a reburial in the family vault. Only as ground in the cemetery is very valuable the management does its best to get the perpetual concessions back into its own hands: it insists that the owner should reaffirm his rights every thirty years. This period had elapsed. We had not been notified in due time that we ran the danger of losing our rights and we therefore still had them—on condition that there was no descendant of the Mignots who might dispute our possession. Until such time as a lawyer should have provided proofs of this, Maman's body would be kept in a repository.

We dreaded the next day's ceremony. We took tranquillizers, slept until seven, drank some tea, ate, and took more tranquillizers. A little before eight a black motor-hearse stopped in the deserted street: before dawn it had gone to fetch the corpse, which had been taken out of the nursing-home by a side-door. We walked through the cold morning fog; we took our seats, Poupette between the driver and one of the Messieurs Durand, I at the back, next to a kind of metal locker. 'Is she there?' asked my sister. 'Yes.' She gave a short sob: 'The only comfort I have,' she said, 'is that it will happen to me too. Otherwise it would be too unfair.' Yes. We were taking part in the dress rehearsal for our own burial. The misfortune is that although everyone must come to this, each experiences the adventure in solitude. We never left Maman during those last days which she confused with convalescence and yet we were profoundly separated from her.

As we drove across Paris I looked at the streets and the people, carefully thinking of nothing. There were cars waiting at the gates of the cemetery: the family. They followed us as far as the chapel. Everybody got out. While the undertaker's men were bringing out the coffin I drew Poupette over towards Maman's sister, whose face was red and swollen with grief. We went in, making a procession: the chapel was full of people. No flowers on the catafalque: the undertakers had left them in the hearse—it did not matter.

A young priest, wearing trousers under his chasuble, celebrated the mass and gave a short, strangely sad sermon. 'God is very far away,' he said. 'Even for those among you whose faith is the strongest there are days when God is so far that He seems not to be there. One might almost say careless. But He has sent us His son.' Two kneeling-chairs had been placed for communion. Almost everybody communicated. The priest spoke again, briefly. And emotion seized both of us by the throat when he said, 'Françoise de Beauvoir'; the words brought her to life; they summed up her history, from birth to marriage, to widowhood, to the grave; Françoise de Beauvoir—that retiring woman, so rarely named—became an important person.

People went by in a line; some of the women were crying. We were still shaking hands when the undertaker's men took the coffin out of the chapel; this time Poupette saw it and she collapsed on my shoulder. 'I had promised her that she shouldn't be put into that box!' I congratulated myself that she did not have that other prayer to remember—'Don't let me fall into the hole!' One of the Messieurs Durand explained to the people there that now they might go away—it was over. The hearse moved off all by itself; I do not even know where it went.

In a blotting-pad that I had brought back from the clinic I found two lines on a narrow piece of paper, written by Maman in a hand as stiff and firm as when she was twenty: 'I should like a very simple funeral. No flowers or

wreaths. But a great many prayers.' Well, we
had carried out her last wishes, and all the more
faithfully since the flowers had been forgotten.

WHY did my mother's death shake me so deeply?
Since the time I left home I had felt little in
the way of emotional impulse towards her.
When she lost my father the intensity and the
simplicity of her sorrow moved me, and so did
her care for others—'Think of yourself,' she said
to me, supposing that I was holding back my
tears so as not to make her suffering worse. A
year later her mother's dying was a painful
reminder of her husband's: on the day of the
funeral a nervous breakdown compelled her to
stay in bed. I spent the night beside her: for-
getting my disgust for this marriage-bed in
which I had been born and in which my father
had died, I watched her sleeping; at fifty-five,
with her eyes closed and her face calm, she was
still beautiful; I wondered that the strength of
her feelings should have overcome her will.
Generally speaking I thought of her with no
particular feeling. Yet in my sleep (although
my father only made very rare and then insig-
nificant appearances) she often played a most
important part: she blended with Sartre, and
we were happy together. And then the dream
would turn into a nightmare: why was I living

with her once more? How had I come to be in
her power again? So our former relationship
lived on in me in its double aspect—a subjection
that I loved and hated. It revived with all its
strength when Maman's accident, her illness
and her death shattered the routine that then
governed our contacts. Time vanishes behind
those who leave this world, and the older I get
the more my past years draw together. The
'Maman darling' of the days when I was ten can
no longer be told from the inimical woman who
oppressed my adolescence; I wept for them
both when I wept for my old mother. I thought
I had made up my mind about our failure and
accepted it; but its sadness comes back to my
heart. There are photographs of both of us,
taken at about the same time: I am eighteen,
she is nearly forty. Today I could almost be her
mother and the grandmother of that sad-eyed
girl. I am so sorry for them—for me because I
am so young and I understand nothing; for her
because her future is closed and she has never
understood anything. But I would not know
how to advise them. It was not in my power
to wipe out the unhappiness in her childhood
that condemned Maman to make me unhappy
and to suffer in her turn from having done so.
For if she embittered several years of my life, I
certainly paid her back though I did not set
out to do so. She was intensely anxious about
my soul. As far as this world was concerned, she
was pleased at my successes, but she was hurt
by the scandal that I aroused among the people
she knew. It was not pleasant for her to hear a
cousin state, 'Simone is the family's disgrace.'

The changes in Maman during her illness made my sorrow all the greater. As I have already said, she was a woman of a strong and eager temperament, and because of her renunciations she had grown confused and difficult. Confined to her bed, she decided to live for herself; and yet at the same time she retained an unvarying care for others—from her conflicts there arose a harmony. My father and his social character coincided exactly: his class and he spoke through his mouth with one identical voice. His last words, 'You began to earn your living very young, Simone: your sister cost me a great deal of money', were not of a kind to encourage tears. My mother was awkwardly laced into a spiritualistic ideology; but she had an animal passion for life which was the source of her courage and which, once she was conscious of the weight of her body, brought her towards truth. She got rid of the ready-made notions that hid her sincere and lovable side. It was then that I felt the warmth of an affection that had often been distorted by jealousy and that she expressed so badly. In her papers I have found touching evidence of it. She had put aside two letters, the one written by a Jesuit and the other by a friend; they both assured her that one day I should come back to God. She had copied out a passage from Chamson in which he says in effect 'If, when I was twenty, I had met an older, highly-regarded man who had talked to me about Nietszche and Gide and freedom, I should have broken with home.' The file was completed by an article cut out of a paper—*Jean-Paul Sartre has saved a soul*. In this

Rémy Roure said—quite untruthfully, by the way—that after *Bariona* had been acted at Stalag xii d an atheistical doctor was converted. I know very well what she wanted from these pieces—it was to be reassured about me; but she would never have felt the need if she had not been intensely anxious as to my salvation. 'Of course I should like to go to Heaven: but not all alone, not without my daughters,' she wrote to a young nun.

Sometimes, though very rarely, it happens that love, friendship or comradely feeling overcomes the loneliness of death: in spite of appearances, even when I was holding Maman's hand, I was not with her—I was lying to her. Because she had always been deceived, gulled, I found this ultimate deception revolting. I was making myself an accomplice of that fate which was so misusing her. Yet at the same time in every cell of my body I joined in her refusal, in her rebellion: and it was also because of that that her defeat overwhelmed me. Although I was not with Maman when she died, and although I had been with three people when they were actually dying, it was when I was at her bedside that I saw Death, the Death of the dance of death, with its bantering grin, the Death of fireside tales that knocks on the door, a scythe in its hand, the Death that comes from elsewhere, strange and inhuman: it had the very face of Maman when she showed her gums in a wide smile of unknowingness.

'He is certainly of an age to die.' The sadness of the old; their banishment: most of them do not think that this age has yet come for them.

I too made use of this cliché, and that when I was referring to my mother. I did not understand that one might sincerely weep for a relative, a grandfather aged seventy and more. If I met a woman of fifty overcome with sadness because she had just lost her mother, I thought her neurotic: we are all mortal; at eighty you are quite old enough to be one of the dead . . .

But it is not true. You do not die from being born, nor from having lived, nor from old age. You die from *something*. The knowledge that because of her age my mother's life must soon come to an end did not lessen the horrible surprise: she had sarcoma. Cancer, thrombosis, pneumonia: it is as violent and unforeseen as an engine stopping in the middle of the sky. My mother encouraged one to be optimistic when, crippled with arthritis and dying, she asserted the infinite value of each instant; but her vain tenaciousness also ripped and tore the reassuring curtain of everyday triviality. There is no such thing as a natural death: nothing that happens to a man is ever natural, since his presence calls the world into question. All men must die: but for every man his death is an accident and, even if he knows it and consents to it, an unjustifiable violation.

SIMONE DE BEAUVOIR has an almost legendary reputation as a writer and "high priestess" of the Existentialist movement in Paris. Since her early twenties, she has been associated intellectually and personally with Jean-Paul Sartre, who later became the major exponent of this movement and one of the world's leading men of letters.

Madame de Beauvoir is best known for *The Mandarins*, which was awarded the Goncourt Prize, and for *The Second Sex*, *Force of Circumstance*, *Memoirs of a Dutiful Daughter*, *The Prime of Life*, and *The Coming of Age*. She is the author of four novels, a play and several volumes of essays.

THE BEST OF BESTSELLERS FROM WARNER BOOKS!

THE BEST OF BESTSELLERS
FROM WARNER BOOKS!